W9-AVM-177

BEST-LOVED STORIES TOLD
AT THE NATIONAL STORYTELLI

C1991

1000060787875609   CENT

Best-Loved
Stories

Told at the
National Storytelling
Festival

Best-Loved
Stories

Told at the National Storytelling Festival

Selected by the
National Association for the
Preservation and Perpetuation of Storytelling

NATIONAL STORYTELLING PRESS
Jonesborough, Tennessee

Distributed to the Book Trade by August House Publishers • P.O. Box 3223 • Little Rock, Ark. 72203

Published by the
National Storytelling Press
of the
National Association for the
Preservation and Perpetuation of Storytelling
P.O. Box 309 ■ Jonesborough, Tenn. 37659 ■ 615-753-2171

Printed in the United States

96 95 94 93 92   5 4 3 2 1

Project direction by Jimmy Neil Smith
Editorial guidance by Mary C. Weaver
Design by Jane L. Hillhouse

Library of Congress Cataloging-in-Publication Data

Best-Loved Stories Told at the National Storytelling Festival/selected by
   the National Association for the Preservation and Perpetuation of
   Storytelling—20th anniversary edition
         p. cm.
      Includes index.
      Summary: A collection of 37 traditional and adapted folk and fairy
   tales, original tales, true narratives, and ghost stories, told at the annual
   National Storytelling Festival from 1973 to 1990. Includes information
   about the storytellers, the tales, and the background of the festival.
      ISBN 1-879991-01-2 (hardcover edition); ISBN 1-879991-00-4
   (softcover edition)
         1. Tales. 2. Tales—United States. 3. National Storytelling Festival.
   [1. Folklore. 2. National Storytelling Festival. 3. Storytelling.]
   I. National Association for the Preservation and Perpetuation of
   Storytelling.
   GR73.B47 1991   91-30058
   398.2—dc20   CIP   AC

To our
storytellers—for sharing
their stories.

CONTENTS

How This Book Came to Be

It was very nearly named the Bugaboo Springs Storytelling Festival, back in early 1973, when the civic leaders of the tiny Tennessee town of Jonesborough contemplated their first storytelling festival. "Is there any other such event held anywhere in the country?" they queried. "None that I know of," answered the high school journalism teacher who had come up with the idea. "Then let's call it the National Storytelling Festival."

The schoolteacher, who later became the town's mayor, was Jimmy Neil Smith, and his inspiration had been a well-told tale heard over a squawking car radio. The story, told by Grand Ole Opry regular Jerry Clower about coon hunting in Mississippi, wasn't particularly awe-inspiring. But it was enough to fire Smith's imagination.

Jerry Clower headlined at that first event, held in a high school gymnasium for a thousand or so attentive listeners. The next day, on an old farm wagon surrounded by bales of hay for bleachers, more stories were told. The next year the telling moved to kitchens and parlors, porches and lawns, scattered throughout historic Jonesborough. This time there was no big-name teller—just a few good folks who could tell a good tale.

By 1975, though, the tellers and the listeners had begun to emerge in unbelievable numbers. Librarians, teachers, and travelers from every location and walk of life were making their way to Jonesborough. Just a few years after its humble beginnings on that hay wagon, the festival, by necessity, moved from porches to meeting halls—and ultimately into large and colorful tents. Now listeners congregate by the thousands each year to hear the ever-widening array of talent. Today the National Storytelling Festival is recognized as the first event of its kind in America and the most prestigious of the scores of festivals that have since sprung up. Its impact on storytelling as a major art form continues to be felt worldwide.

While staging a major storytelling event was significant in rekindling the storytelling tradition in America, it's what happened two years later that made possible a true revival of the art. In 1975, at the conclusion of the third National Storytelling Festival, founder Jimmy Neil Smith called together a few of the tellers who had nurtured the festival. "Let's think about forming an association," he said simply, "to support storytelling and storytellers." And that very weekend he, along with six others, named a board of directors, adopted a set of bylaws, and created the National Association for the Preservation and Perpetuation of Storytelling (NAPPS).

Over the years the organization has grown from a handful of supporters to more than 5,000 dues-paying members, representing all 50 states and two dozen foreign countries. It's through the networking and connecting influences of the association that storytelling is gaining momentum as a respected art form in modern America.

The 1992 National Storytelling Festival marks the 20th anniversary of this internationally acclaimed event. To commemorate this milestone in the history of America's storytelling renaissance, NAPPS's National Storytelling Press has published this book: *Best-Loved Stories Told at the National Storytelling Festival*. This anthology's 37 tales make up a sampler drawn from the hundreds of stories that have been told on crisp October days and nights in Jonesborough since the festival's inception.

Best-Loved Stories Told at the National Storytelling Festival honors 20 years of storytelling—two decades of voices, reverberating with thousands of years of memories and dreams and history. But just as important, this collection pays homage to the storytellers, who with their stories have given us wisdom, joy, and hope. Truly this is something to celebrate.

MY STORY, YOUR STORY, OUR STORY—HISTORY

An introduction by Jane Yolen

I spent a semester, not too long ago, living in Scotland, where every cobblestone bleeds stories, and every stone on the mountainside tells a tale. One cannot walk along the streets of Edinburgh without coming upon a narrative: here 27 Covenanters died for their beliefs; there resurrection men plied their ghastly midnight trade; on this very spot Lord Darnley killed poor Riccio and dragged his corpse along the floor. See? The bloodstains have not come clean!

On the Highland hills a wild stag suddenly leaps up, his does behind him, and every line of Scottish poetry I have ever known seems to sing down the braes. In Dunvegan Castle on the Isle of Skye there hangs a tattered remnant of cloth called the Fairy Flag, with two lines written below it to tell you why. On a wind- and rain-swept moor I can swear I hear the skirling ghosts of pipers, sounding the death knell of the clans. Closing my eyes to slits, I can see the fatal hesitation that broke the ranks at Culloden. And so on and so on.

I mulled over those tales and those settings for months because it seemed to me that in some places of the world—certainly in Scotland— people live closer to the story that lies within the word *history*. And surely they are made stronger by their association with the past. Their ghosts are not dead but alive, not stuck in the musty long ago but breathing beside them.

As the French philosopher Montaigne once proclaimed, "We are, I know not how, two souls in a single breast." Those souls are Then and Now. Yesterday and This Moment. What Was and What Is. And surely it is story that provides the lifeline between.

When I returned to America at Christmastime, stuffed full of such stories as "The Fairy Flag" and "Tam Lin" and "The Kintail Witches," I realized how bereft of tales we are in this country. Oh, the stories are here—the stories of Jack and Br'er Rabbit and Coyote and Raven and all the other tricksters. But for so long we had made our ghosts mute—or pushed them back into the nursery closet. After all, America was founded on a retreat from the past, a breaking with tradition, a searching for the new.

In New York City, where I grew up, old buildings are torn down faster than new ones can be built. P.S. 93, where I learned multiplication and kissing, is now a parking lot. The ballet school where I sweated onto the barre has given way to a high-rise bank. And when the new buildings go up, they take the place—heart, soul, mortar, and cement—of dozens of old ones. Then all the stories in those torn-down structures are lost; all the voices are ground into the unforgiving pavement.

Even in the countryside, where I now live, shopping malls with little history and with stories produced only by celluloid strips and computer chips in the video arcades are taking the place of farms where tales were told around the hearth-fire on winter nights and swamps where Br'er Frog used to sing his busy chorus into the summer night.

In our schools oral history is forgotten in the rush to make our children semiliterate and semi-articulate (and let TV and computers do the rest!), while those written-down stories we do offer them are most often bowdlerized and sanitized and censored by politically correct critics on the left and religious fanatics on the right and well-meaning, scared citizens in the middle. When you catch me at my grumpiest, I will most likely rant that we are developing a nation of readers whose only reading material is bumper stickers, buttons, and bookmarks—the Three B's instead of the Three R's. And, I will add, whose only acquaintance with story—our human heritage—is the stand-up comic's routine.

Thank God, then, for the hardy band of storytellers who go to schools and libraries and hospitals and coffeehouses and concert halls and nursing homes and conventions and simply . . . eloquently . . . passionately . . . coolly . . . tell stories.

Humans are the animals that tell stories. This characteristic defines us more clearly than the opposable thumb. Wolves in their packs wag their tails and point their ears, but they do not tell tales. Dolphins click and clatter, but they do not render sagas. Whales may sing, but their message is sonar, not story. Chickens communicate a pecking order, not an epic order. Only human beings tell tales.

In our stories we entertain, but we also inform, teach, establish moral precedents, record history, remind ourselves of genealogy, lay down laws. Story is a mnemonic device that by its very memorability reminds us of what we already know: we are human. We thrive in human society. Whatever our differences, we are the same. However much we are the same, we are different as well.

Children learn by story. Red Riding Hood warns of the cozening stranger; Br'er Rabbit tells us the bully can be defeated; Raven says that there is a necessary chaos in the world's order. But adults learn from stories as well: "Carna and the Boots of Seven Strides" reminds us that women can be heroes too; "No News," that both optimism and pessimism have alternatives; "The Seal Skin," that keeping secrets from our families is a dangerous business. Sometimes a story is just plain fun, and that's all right too!

The stories in this book were set down for you out of the mouths of the tellers—no simple task. But that is not the entire history of the stories here. Some were first learned from pages, some went the traditional mouth-to-ear route of the oldest tales, some were learned from records and tapes, and some are original creations. In any case, stories, to stay alive, must be transmitted.

But are stories on the page the same as stories in the mouth? Yes and no.

The written story comes to one quietly, often under the covers; it paces beneath the hand. It has time for slow flourishes. It can be returned to as easily as the page is turned back. It is memory codified.

The oral tale flashes by, and one can be turned off or turned on by the accomplished teller as much as by the tale. It changes at every telling. It is bare-boned, refined to its essence, polished by a succession of tongues. In some sense it is more immediately manipulative.

Though the written and oral story are different, they have similarities too. A story has power over life. Each telling—on the page or in the mouth—defines the reader or listener to himself. The act of reading a story or listening to it is a taking-in of the story's power. The story transforms, changes, and transfigures the one who takes it in.

Nearly two decades ago, when the National Storytelling Festival was born, storytelling was kept minimally alive in America by a few backcountry tellers, a few front-porch tellers, a few hearth-fire tellers at family camps—and librarians, bless them, holding story hours. Today 500 tellers are listed in the *National Directory of Storytelling* (a publication of the National Association for the Preservation and Perpetuation of Storytelling), and they represent only a fraction of the professional storytellers in this country. *But this is not enough.* All humans have the potential for storytelling. Perhaps this book of stories will help liberate them. All humans have stories inside them, waiting to be told.

No, make that: All humans are stories waiting to be told. My story, your story, our story—history.

Hatfield, Massachusetts

THE WISH-RING

Martha Holloway

There was once a young farmer who, in spite of his hard work and honest ways, remained poor. One day as he was resting from his plowing, eating his lunch of bread and cheese under the shade of a tree, he saw coming down the road an old bent-over woman, barely able to put one foot in front of the other. She stared hungrily at the farmer's food. He said to her, "Come, Old Mother, and rest a while. I will share my bread and cheese."

She sat and ate and was refreshed, and as she stood to go, she said, "Because of your kindness I wish to help you. Walk two days till you come to a great fir tree that stands in the forest and overtops all the other trees. If you can hew it down, you will make your fortune."

The farmer shouldered his ax and started on his journey at once. Sure enough, after tramping for two days, he came to the fir tree and began to chop. The tree began to sway, and just before it fell with a crash, out of its branches dropped a nest that held two eggs. The eggs fell to the ground and broke. Out of one darted a young eagle, and out of the other rolled a gold ring. The eagle spread its wings and, soaring upward, cried, "Take the ring. It is a wish-ring. Turn it on your finger twice, and whatever you wish, it shall be fulfilled. But remember, there is but a single wish in the ring. No sooner is that wish granted than the ring loses its power and becomes an ordinary ring. Therefore, consider well what you desire so that you may never have reason to repent your choice."

The farmer took the ring, placed it on his finger, and made his way homeward. Toward evening he reached a town, and as he walked through it, he saw a jeweler sitting in his shop, behind a counter on which lay many costly rings for sale. Curious about what the merchant would say the value of his new ring was, the farmer asked, "How much do you think this is worth?"

"Not a straw," the jeweler answered.

The farmer laughed. "This ring is of greater value than all the rings in your shop put together. It's a wish-ring."

Barbara Snow of Eugene, Oregon, gave me this story to tell for the 50th wedding anniversary of a North Dakota farm couple. In their own hands lay the magic of honest work, undergirded by their belief in a power they could call on if necessary. The tale will appear in Storytelling Treasures From St. Nicholas Magazine, *compiled by Barbara Snow and Paulette Thompson.*

17

The jeweler was a wicked, designing man. He said to the farmer, "Why don't you rest from your journey and stay the night with me. Sheltering a man who owns a wish-ring will bring me luck."

He treated his guest to fair words, fine food, and much wine. And that night as the farmer lay sound asleep, the wicked jeweler stole the magic ring from his finger and slipped on, in its place, a common ring that he had made to look like the magic one.

As soon as the farmer continued his journey the next morning, the jeweler closed his shop, put up the shutters so that no one could peep in, and bolted the door. Standing in the middle of the room, he turned the ring and cried, "I wish for a million gold pieces!"

No sooner had he said the words than great shining gold pieces came pouring down upon him in a torrent over his head and shoulders and arms. Before he could unbar the door, the weight of the gold crushed him and broke the floor, and the jeweler and his money sank through to the cellar. The noise alarmed the neighbors, and they came rushing over. When they found the man dead under his gold, they exclaimed, "Doubly unfortunate is he whom blessings kill."

Afterward the jeweler's heirs came and divided the property.

In the meantime, the farmer reached home in high spirits and showed the ring to his wife. "Henceforth we shall never be in want. Only we must be very careful to consider well just what we ought to wish."

"Well," she said, "suppose we wish for that bit of land that lies between our two fields."

"That isn't worthwhile," the husband said. "If we work hard for a year, we'll earn enough money to buy it."

So the two worked very hard, and at harvest time they had raised such a crop as never before. They had earned enough money to buy the land and still had a bit to spare.

"See," said the man, "we have the land and the wish as well."

The wife then said, "We really need a cow and a horse. What would you think of wishing for them?"

"Oh, no. Let's not waste it on trifles," he said. "We will manage to get the horse and cow."

And in a year's time they had saved the money for the horse and cow. Joyfully the man rubbed his hands. "The wish is saved again, and yet we have what we desire. How lucky we are!"

"Yes, dear husband, but there's something we don't have—children. I do long for children. Could we use the wish for such a blessing?"

"I too want children. But let's be patient for a while longer and see if God will bless us."

And the next year they were overjoyed to have a baby son and in the years after, five more healthy children.

But now the farmer's wife talked seriously about using the wish at last. "You slave and toil when you might be a gentleman with chests overflowing with gold. Or a baron. Or even a king."

And he answered, "We are still young, and life is long. There is only one wish in the ring, and who knows when we may sorely need it. Are we in want for anything? Have we not prospered to all people's astonishment since we possessed this ring? Be reasonable and patient for a while."

And that was the end of the matter. It really seemed as if the ring had brought a blessing into the house. The farmer's granaries and barns were full to overflowing, and in the course of a few years he became a rich man. Still he worked with his men in the fields as if he too had to earn his daily bread.

And so the years went by. Sometimes when they were alone, the farmer's wife would remind her husband of the magic ring and suggest many plans. But he always answered that they had plenty of time and that the best thoughts come last. Finally, she stopped speaking of it altogether.

To be sure, the farmer looked at the ring and twirled it about as many as 20 times a day, but he was very careful never to wish. After many years had passed, the farmer and his wife had grown old, and their wish was still unasked. Then was God very good to them, and on the same night both of them died peacefully.

Their weeping children and grandchildren gathered 'round the two coffins. One daughter wanted to remove the ring from the still hand of her father as a remembrance. But the oldest son said, "Let our father take his ring into the grave. There was always a mystery about it. Our mother often looked at the ring. Perhaps she gave it to him when they were young."

So the old farmer was buried with the ring that had been supposed to be a wish-ring and was not. Yet it brought as much good fortune as any heart could desire.

Martha Holloway of La Jolla, California, is a retired bacteriologist who began a second career as a professional storyteller at age 62. That was more than a decade ago, and Holloway has since developed a national reputation as a teller of folk tales and Appalachian stories.

THE WALKIN' CATFISH

Doc McConnell

I's raised over there at Stoney Point, close to Tucker's Knob. Seem like all I ever done was hoe corn or fish, and I fished as much as I could.

One day I was down there at John Mauk's ol' mill pond a-fishin', a-catchin' catfish. I's catchin' them fish as fast as I could—pullin' 'em out one right after the other. I was throwin' 'em over there on the bank behind me. After a while they quit bitin', and I commenced to stringin' 'em up. All of 'em had done died and got stiff, lyin' there in the hot sun, except one ol' catfish. He was goin' WHISH OO, WHISH OO, WHISH OO, still a-breathin'. Well, I just hung him on my stringin' line and went on to the house.

I started to clean them fish, but I tossed the ol' fish that was still a-breathin' over in the grass. The next mornin' that old fish was still a-livin'. You know, I struck up an idea. I just thought I'd start trainin' that ol' fish.

I fixed him up a bucket of water, and I took him out of the water about two hours the first day and about three hours the second day and about four hours the next day, and I kep' on a-workin' with him and a-workin' with him until I left him out all mornin'. Finally, I left him out all day long. It wasn't long before that fish had learned to stay out of the water completely and never went near the water at all.

That ol' fish was the finest pet a boy ever had. I named him Homer. I put a little string 'round him and led him 'round like a little ol' dog and taught him to follow me. He just wiggled through the gravel and dirt and followed me ever'where I went. Never did I go anywhere unless ol' Homer would go with me. Homer followed me ever'where.

I kep' ol' Homer 'round all summer long until school took up in the fall. And when I left the house for school each mornin', ol' Homer followed me right on down the road, just a-waggin' in the dirt. I would throw rocks at him to try to get him to go back to the house, but he wouldn't go.

One day as I was walkin' to school, I kep' a-lookin' over my shoulder, and he was still a-wigglin' there in the dirt, a-followin' me down the road.

I grew up in rural Tennessee. The only book we had to read at our old log-cabin home was the Bible, and once in a while we saw a two-day-old newspaper at the general store. If we wanted to be entertained and informed, we told stories. This is a traditional Southern Appalachian tale I heard from my brother, Steamer.

I got almost up to the schoolhouse, and as I crossed a little wooden bridge over a little creek, I looked back, and ol' Homer was nowhere in sight.

I couldn't see him nowhere. I went back there and begun lookin' around that bridge, and there was a board that had broken and rotted and fell off that bridge. I looked down there through that hole, and there ol' Homer lay in the water, drowned.

Doc McConnell grew up in Tucker's Knob, Tennessee, hearing and swapping tales at John Mauk's country store. Now of Rogersville, Tennessee, he went on to create Doc McConnell's Old-Time Medicine Show, which he has performed for audiences throughout America.

THE HOLE THAT WILL NOT STAY FILLED

Kathryn Windham

Nobody has ever actually seen the ghost of Bill Sketoe, but people going along the road from Newton near where the old bridge crossed the Choctawhatchee River can tell that the ghost has been there. Invariably, the hole under the tree where Sketoe was hanged is clean, as clean as if a brush broom or a pine top had swept it out.

Even if the hole is heaped high with dirt during the day, the dirt disappears during the night, and the next morning the hole is there again.

Bill Sketoe, whose ghost is believed to keep the hole cleaned out, was born in Madrid, Spain, on June 8, 1818. When he was just a little lad, he came with his father to Dale County and settled near Newton, a small town in the Wiregrass section of Alabama. There were not many Spaniards in that part of the country, and some people were suspicious of foreigners. But Bill was a good boy who won the respect of his neighbors, and when he grew up, he became a Methodist minister.

After he entered the ministry, Sketoe became known as "the Bible-reading preacher from Spain," and he was invited to preach at churches throughout the area. He was made pastor of a log-cabin Methodist church at Newton, and he was a kind pastor as well as a powerful preacher. It was while he was preaching at Newton that he met and married an attractive girl, and the two built a home in the community.

When the Civil War began in 1861, Sketoe was one of the first men from his county to join the Confederate Army. He fought bravely for three years in the thick of many battles, almost miraculously escaping serious injury. Then in the fall of 1864 he received a message that his wife was very sick.

Having come from a country so far away from Alabama, Sketoe had no relatives to turn to for help. His wife didn't have any close relatives either, at least none whom Sketoe felt he could ask to stay with her in Newton to nurse her.

He decided that the only thing he could do was hire a substitute to

Folklorist Margaret Figh told me the story of the 1864 hanging of Bill Sketoe and the hole that marks the spot where he died. The story, handed down in the oral tradition, is also well-documented historically. It has drama, truth, and wonder—the perfect ingredients for a ghost story. No wonder I like to tell it.

take his place in the Army so that he could go home and take care of his wife. Now, it wasn't at all unusual for Confederate soldiers to pay other men to fight in their place during times of personal emergency. The asking price for a substitute was about a thousand dollars—a lot of money for a rural Methodist minister turned soldier—but somehow Sketoe managed to scrape up the needed cash.

As soon as his substitute reported for duty, Sketoe jumped on his horse and headed for Newton, making the trip back home in near-record time. His wife was so glad to see her husband and so relieved to have him home that she began to improve immediately. But her long illness had left her weak and frail, and Sketoe felt he should stay with her until she regained her strength.

The threat of defeat hung heavily over the South in 1864, and the Confederacy was in desperate need of every soldier it could get. Under the circumstances, Sketoe's prolonged stay at home began to arouse some resentment and suspicion among the locals. A few of his neighbors, who knew Sketoe was a foreigner, began to wonder if he might not be a traitor as well.

At Newton a number of men had organized themselves to round up and punish deserters. They called themselves Captain Brear's Home Guard. Some people had made accusations that the guard had been organized for the purpose of keeping its members safe at home while other men were fighting for the South, but the unit's defenders said its members were really too old or infirm to serve in the military forces and that they performed a commendable service for the Confederacy.

In any event, the guard heard about Sketoe's return from the Army, came to the conclusion that he was a traitor, and made plans to ambush him and give him a deserter's punishment. On the evening of December 3, 1864, members of the Home Guard gathered at the foot of the bridge on the west side of the Choctawhatchee River to waylay their victim.

When Sketoe appeared, two men engaged him in conversation, and Sketoe responded gratefully to their apparent gesture of friendship. He answered their questions about his wife's health and even showed them the medicine he had gone to town to purchase for her.

As they talked, the other men, who had been hiding in a thicket of huckleberry bushes, crept up behind Sketoe and slipped a noose of new rope around his neck. Sketoe was a big, strong man, but he had been treacherously surprised. Although he struggled valiantly to escape, it was to no purpose. His captors pinioned his arms to his back by a tight cord and tied his feet together. Then they shoved him to the ground and took turns kicking him as they forced him to crawl in the deep sand.

Tiring of this sport and wishing to get on with the punishment they had planned, the members of the "military court" threw Sketoe into a buggy and maneuvered the vehicle to a spot underneath a stout limb jutting out from the south side of a big post-oak tree. This was to be Sketoe's hanging tree.

At that moment Wesley Dowling, who knew and admired Sketoe, came down the road. When he saw what was happening, he stopped and began to beg the Home Guard to give their captive a fair trial. Instead of listening to his plea, one of the men gave Dowling a hard cuff and threatened to hang him too if he interfered further.

Alarmed, lest other passersby should see what they were up to, the men in the guard hastened their preparations for Sketoe's hanging. They threw the rope over the limb and then asked Sketoe if he had any last words. He replied that he would like to pray. That made the men a little uneasy, but how could they refuse to let a man have a final prayer, particularly if he was a preacher? So they granted his request. But instead of praying for himself, as they had expected, Sketoe prayed for his tormentors.

"Forgive them, dear Lord. Forgive them," he prayed.

This so infuriated the Home Guard that even before the doomed man had finished praying, Captain Brear gave a sharp lash of his whip to the rump of the red horse hitched to the buggy. The frightened animal plunged forward, jerking Sketoe out of the buggy.

But Sketoe's neck wasn't broken. In making their hurried plans for the hanging, the Home Guard members hadn't allowed for their victim's height and size. Sketoe was tall, and his frame was not spare. So the limb to which the rope was tied bent under Sketoe's weight, and his toes touched the ground.

Quickly, George Echols, a cripple, grabbed his crutch and used it to dig a hole in the sandy soil under Sketoe's feet so that his toes would not touch the ground and his body would swing from the rope. Finally, the noose tightened and did its deadly work.

News of what was happening near the bridge reached Newton too late for the minister's friends to save his life, but several men went to the spot, took Sketoe's body down from the tree, and laid it out in a cotton house across the road. He was later buried in the graveyard at Mount Carmel Church, where his tombstone may be seen today.

But the story of Bill Sketoe did not end with his burial. The six men who had hanged him were never able to sleep peacefully at night after that, and not one of them would walk alone outside after dark. Though they locked their doors and barred their windows, they were tormented by dread and fear. And each one of the six in his turn met a violent death.

One was killed on horseback when a limb from a post-oak tree, the same kind of tree on which Sketoe was hung, fell on him. It was a still day with not a breath of wind stirring, but the heavy limb fell just as the rider passed beneath the tree. Another member of the lynch mob was killed when thrown from a runaway mule that unaccountably took fright on a quiet, open stretch of road. A third member of the group was struck by lightning, and one was found dead in a deep swamp. The other two also met their death in mysterious ways.

Almost immediately after the hanging, curious people began visiting the site of the tragedy. As time went by, they observed that the hole dug by the crutch did not fill up as an ordinary hole would have, and people whispered that Sketoe's ghost was returning to the spot to keep the hole clean.

Some years later two men who were part of a crew that was building a new bridge over the river decided to camp on the spot where Sketoe had died. They did not believe in ghosts, so they filled up the hole and pitched their tent over it. The braver of the two men put his bedroll directly over the freshly filled hole, and they spent a fairly comfortable night.

Next morning when they broke camp, the braver man picked up his bedroll and found to his amazement that the hole was there again, although he had filled it up himself and lain on it all night long.

The hanging oak isn't there anymore, but the hole still is. It is about 30 inches wide at the top and slopes to a depth of about eight inches. Three young pine trees now grow close to the hole, but even their needles do not remain in it. Something sweeps them away, leaving the hole as clean and as empty as it was the day an innocent man was hanged there.

Kathryn Windham of Selma, Alabama, has collected Southern tales, including true ghost stories, for more than 50 years. She is the author of 16 books, including 13 Southern Ghosts *and* Jeffrey.

Could This Be Paradise?

Steve Sanfield

Once when I was 12 years old, I whined to my grandfather about my situation in life. Nothing, absolutely nothing, was right. While I went on and on with my litany of complaints, my grandfather listened with what I now think was infinite patience. When I had finished, he said, "Stevela, let me tell you a story," and he told me this tale.

There was once a man who was unhappy with his life. Nothing seemed to be right. He had to work much too hard for far too little. Neither his friends nor his neighbors gave him the respect he felt he deserved. His wife was always complaining, and his children were never satisfied.

Despite his hopes, his condition did not improve, so he spent most of his time dreaming about Paradise. Whether he was alone or with others, whether at work or at rest, the idea of Paradise filled his head. "Someday," he kept telling himself, "someday I'm going to go to Paradise."

And one day—no different from any other—he decided that this was the day he was going to set off for Paradise.

Rising from his morning table, without saying a word to his wife and his two children, he went out the front door, past the gate with the broken latch, and through the open fields, until he came to the edge of the marketplace. He already knew which women would buy what goods from which merchants at what price and what they would argue about. He passed a bakery opposite a butcher shop, went on through the center of town with its synagogue and town hall, and continued out through another set of fields to the base of a long, steep hill.

He climbed the hill until he reached the beginning of a broad plateau. There he paused and took one last look at his village below. He was sure he would never see it again. He was a man bound for Paradise.

All day he walked along that plateau, and when the sun was setting in the west, he decided to take shelter under a tall pine tree. Before going to sleep, he removed his shoes and pointed them in the direction he was sure Paradise lay.

But how was he to know that in the darkest hour of the night a demon, an imp, would come and—either to punish him or to save him or to teach him a lesson or maybe just to play a joke on him—take his shoes and turn them around? No way for the man to know that.

The next morning the man rose early, said his prayers, and stepped into his shoes, certain that they would lead him to Paradise. Off he went, his head filled with dreams. Suddenly, there he was at the edge of the plateau, and just below him, Paradise. He had arrived.

Strange, he thought, *it's not much bigger than my own village. Oh well.*

He descended the hill and walked through the fields to the center of town. Here in Paradise there were also a synagogue and a town hall. As he stood there looking at them, the man thought, *They've been lying to me all these years—or at least exaggerating. They said that everything in Paradise would shine and gleam, but these buildings, why, they're almost as shabby as those in my own village.*

He passed a bakery that stood opposite a butcher shop. He began to suspect that when he entered the marketplace, he would know which women would buy what goods from which merchants at what price and what they would argue about—and he did.

Now more sad than angry, he was sure that if he continued through the fields in front of him, he would come to a gate with a broken latch—and he did.

As he stood there pondering his situation, he heard a whining voice from the house. "Come in and eat your food."

It was enough to drive a man mad. It sounded just like his own wife. But never having said no to his wife and being a bit hungry, he went into the house. He sat down, ate some black bread and some herring, and had a cup of coffee.

Two children came running up to him and jumped into his lap. Playing with his beard, the youngest one asked, "You'll stay with us this time, won't you, Papa?"

Not wanting to say no to the children, he agreed.

And to this very day, that man sits at that table every morning, drinking his coffee, trying to figure out whether he's in Paradise.

Steve Sanfield is an award-winning author and poet. The founder and artistic director of the Sierra Storytelling Festival, Sanfield became the first full-time storyteller in residence in the United States in 1976. He lives outside Nevada City, California.

THE BEE, THE HARP, THE MOUSE, AND THE BUMCLOCK

Gwenda LedBetter

Once there was a widow, and she had a son named Jack. They lived in Ireland, and they lived happily enough, though all they had to their name was three cows. But then, as it happens in life, the potato crop failed. Hard times came, and poverty looked in the door. Things got so bad, the widow said to Jack, "You'll have to take the branny cow to town tomorrow, Jack, and bring home something to lift my heart entirely!"

"Never say it twice, Mother," said Jack, throwing his hand to his hat. The next morning Jack took a stick in his fist, turned out the branny cow, and off to town he went.

At the top of the hill over the town Jack stopped and looked. There was a great crowd of people all gathered in a circle. Being a curious lad, Jack went down and looked in. There was a wee man—no taller than he ought to be, a lot smaller than he should be. He had a green jacket, a red hat, a twinkle in his eye, and the strangest assortment of animals you ever did see. There was a bee, a plain ordinary bee, but it had a harp, an Irish one, of course. There were a mouse and a bumclock. The last you may not be knowing, so I'll tell you that it's nothing in the world but a cockroach.

The wee man set the animals down upon the ground and started in patting his foot. The bee began to play the harp, the mouse and the bumclock took hold of each other like they hadn't seen the other for a couple of weeks, and

> The pots, the pans, the wheels and reels,
> Jack and the cow, the men, the women,
> The boys, the girls, the trees in the street
> All began to jump and jig and dance about.
> Inside in, outside out, all over the place they went—
> You never saw such a sight in your life!

As quickly as he had put them down, the wee man picked up his

I found this tale, collected by Seumas MacManus, in Donegal Fairy Stories during my time of telling stories at the Pack Library of Asheville, North Carolina. The wee man who tricks Jack reminded me of a small man in a Virginia town who teased me out of my loneliness by means of stories. For me he was magic, and so is this tale.

31

animals and put them in his pocket. Then everyone stood around and laughed. And laughed. And laughed. They laughed as long and as loud as they had danced. The wee man turned to Jack, and the twinkle in his eye fairly blazed. "Good morning to you, Jack. How would you like to have these animals?"

"Oh," said Jack, wiping tears from his eyes. "I'd like it fine, I would. That's a grand group, that is."

"Well, then," said the man, "What have you got to bargain with?"

"I've got no money," said Jack. "All I've got is this cow, and I've brought her to town to sell so I can lift my mother's heart entirely."

"Well!" said the wee one, "I'll give you the bee and harp for your very fine cow, and your mother will laugh if she never laughed in all her life before."

"Well, then," said Jack, with the laughter still in him, "That would be grand." He handed over the cow. The wee man went off with her with a gleam in his eye, and Jack went home with a bee and a harp in his pocket.

When he got home, the widow was in the kitchen, peeling the last potato they had to their name. Over her shoulder she called, "Did you sell the cow, Jack?"

"Aye, Mother, I did."

"Good boy. How much money did you get?"

"I didn't exactly get money . . . but I got value."

"What are you sayin', Jack?" His mother turned. Jack put the bee and his harp down on the floor. The bee gave a slap to his Irish cap and started to play and

> *The pots, the pans, the wheels and reels,*
> *Jack and his mother, the table, the chair,*
> *The pot on the hearth, the house itself*

All began to jump and jig and dance about.
Inside in, outside out, all over the place they went—
You never saw such a sight in your life!

When Jack saw his mother's face getting over-red, he picked up the bee, and they laughed. And laughed. And laughed as long and as loud as they had danced. But then the widow gave herself a shake.

"Jack," said she, "You've done a stupid thing. Trading my good branny cow for a bee! It's a talented little fellow, but we've nothing to eat. We can't have bee and harp or the music he makes for supper! You'll have to take my black cow to town tomorrow and bring home something to lift my heart entirely!"

"Never say it twice, Mother," said Jack, said he, throwing his hand to his hat. And in the morning he turned out the black cow, and off to town he went.

When he got there, what did he see—you're not surprised a bit, are you?—but a great crowd of people gathered into a circle. And there was the wee man with the mouse and the bumclock, which he set down on the ground. He began to pat his foot, and

The pots, the pans, the wheels and reels,
Jack and the cow, the men, the women,
The boys and girls, the dogs and cats, and the trees in the street
All began to jump and jig and dance about.
Inside in, outside out, all over the place they went—
You never saw such a dancing time in all your life!

And when the wee man picked up his animals, the people laughed. And laughed. And laughed. They laughed as long and as loud as they had danced, and the wee man turned to Jack.

"Good morning to you, Jack. I'm glad to see you, and how would you like to have the rest of these animals?"

"I'd like it fine, but I cannot."

"Why cannot ye?"

"I promised my mother . . . "

"Ah, but your mother will laugh if she never laughed in all her life if you take home this mouse."

Jack wanted the mouse so bad, he turned the black cow over to the wee man and went home with a mouse in his pocket! When he got home, his mother was sitting on the porch. No more potatoes to peel.

"Well, Jack, did you sell the cow?"

"Aye, Mother, I did."

"How much money did you get?"

"Well, now, Mother . . . "

"Oh, no! Not again!"

Jack whipped the wee animals out of his pocket and put them down. Then he started to pat his foot. The bee began to play. The mouse danced all by himself, and the pots and pans and wheels and reels were grand, entirely.

The laughing went on twice as long as it had the day before, but his mother soon got hold of herself. "You've done it again, Jack. We've nothing to eat in the house, and you bring home another *mouse* to feed!

"There's nothing to be done but you'll have to take the spotted cow and sell her—AND BRING HOME SOMETHING TO LIFT MY HEART ENTIRELY—or I don't know what we'll do."

"Yes, Mother," Jack meekly said.

The next morning he stood on the hill looking down into town, the spotted cow beside him. And there, of course, was the great crowd of people.

"I wonder what they're looking at?" Jack asked the cow. The cow, being a sensible beast, did not say a word. When they went down, the wee man was there with just the brave bumclock, and when the dancing and laughing were over, he said, "Jack, you'd better have this bumclock, for it's a very fine thing to have!"

"I can't!" gasped Jack, looking with longing at the wee thing.

"Well, now, Jack, if you take home the bumclock, your mother will laugh, and you'll have the whole set!"

It was too much for Jack. The wee man went off with the last cow, and Jack went home with a bumclock in his pocket. The widow was at the gate. "Jack! Did you sell the cow?"

"Aye, Mother, I did!"

"Show me the color of your money, boy!"

Jack whipped out all the animals, and right proud he was of the way they danced. The pots and pans all did their thing, and for a moment, the whole world was full of joy. But then Jack looked over to see his mother down on the ground, apron over her head, crying her eyes out. Jack took himself out to the road, sat down on a stone, and said to himself, "How can you do it to your own mother?"

Now, along down the road came an old woman. She was bent to the ground with age, shaped almost in a circle. If you'd tapped her with a stick, she would have rolled.

"Good morning to you, Jack. What are you doin' here? Why aren't you off trying for the princess's hand in marriage?"

"What are you talkin' about, Good Mother?"

"Why, the King of Ireland has a daughter who hasn't laughed for seven years. He says that anyone who can get three laughs out of her will have half of his kingdom and her hand in marriage as well."

"If that's true, it's not here I should be!" said Jack, said he. He kissed the old woman, straightening her back forever. He ran into the house, put his animals in his pocket, put on his old raggedy hat, said, "Goodbye, Mother, I'll see you soon!" and off he went down the road.

Now, when he got to the castle, Jack put his heels to the ground, so to speak. There were sharp stakes up all around the castle, and stuck on top of each stake was a human head. They wore various expressions, but none of them were pleasant. Jack felt a great tightening around his collar. He spoke to a guard standing near.

"Whose—I say—whose heads might those be?"

"Them's the ones who come and tried for the princess's hand—and failed!"

"A mighty big crowd!" said Jack, said he. But he sent word that another had come. The king, the queen, the princess, and all the court came out and sat in little golden chairs, waiting for another beheading. Jack took his animals out of his pocket, tied a string to them, and taking the end in his hand, walked in front of that grand company. They took a look at raggedy Jack and his tiny animals and began to laugh. The princess turned to see what they were laughing at, and when she saw Jack and his menagerie, she laughed so loud you could hear her in Dublin.

"That's one part of you won, my lady!" said Jack, making a low bow. He took the string away, gave a stone to the bee to sit upon, and with a "Do your stuff, fellows," stepped back. The bee gave a slap to his Irish cap, and lifting his wings, sat down concert-style. The mouse and the bumclock dropped low bows, relatively speaking, to that grand company. Then they took hold of each other like they hadn't seen the other one for 99 years. And

The pots, the pans, the wheels and reels,
Jack and the queen, the king and the court, the castle itself
All began to jump and jig and dance about.
Inside in, outside out, upside-down and all about,
All over the place they went—
You never saw such a dancin' time in all your life!

When the princess saw all that hip-swinging and foot-slinging, she laughed loud enough to be heard in Londontown, and Jack said, without missing a step, "That's two parts of you won, my lady!"

Well, the music kept playing, and the people kept dancing, but there was no more laughing. Jack was feeling very warm around the collar, when the wee mouse did a fancy turn, swept its tail through the bumclock's mouth, and the wee bug started to cough.

"Eeeeh! Eeeeh! Eeeeh!"

I don't know if you've ever seen a cockroach cough. You must know it's a comical thing to see. The princess laughed. And laughed. And laughed so loud, you couldn't hear her at all, but the laugh went all 'round the world, gathering joy as it went, came back, and knocked everyone off his feet!

Jack got up, brushed himself off, wiped his brow, and said, "That's three parts of you won, my lady. I have you all!" And when she saw him dressed in white satin, she said, "I won't mind having him for a husband, at all, at all."

Jack sent for his mother right away. The bee, the mouse, and the bumclock played the music for the wedding, which lasted nine days and nine nights.

I was there myself. That's how I got this story. They gave me brogues, broth, slippers of bread, and I came home dancing on my head!

Gwenda LedBetter was trained as a teacher and a singer but became a storyteller instead. A native of Asheville, North Carolina, LedBetter has shared her folk and spiritual narratives with audiences for more than 25 years.

A Friend of My Father

Maggi Kerr Peirce

When I attended university in early 1980, I took a course in autobiography. On the first day of class the professor told us he expected a story from us every week. We all groaned. In irritation he said, "Come, come—I'm only asking for an anecdote!" This story was the first one read aloud in class and the beginning of my Belfast series.

During the Second World War my father, who was a member of the Royal Ulster Constabulary in Northern Ireland, spent most of his days, and ofttimes nights, at the entrance to the Belfast Harbour Commission. There he perused with solemn dignity all cars and identity cards that moved back and forth in that military-inspected zone. It was a serious job, but to us, his two wee daughters, such work was fraught not with peril but with stories of adventure and humor, with which he would regale us nightly.

One of our favorite tales was about a man with whom Daddy worked. His name was William Dynes, but throughout our childhood he was known as "Stinker" Dynes, and we would wheedle our father into telling us of Stinker's latest escapade.

Now, I must explain that these stories would have been normal, if not downright dull, without the use of Stinker's favorite adjective—but this would be the kind of monologue Daddy would retell:

"'Augh, hello, Billy,' says Stinker Dynes to me, comin' in the back door of the Nissen hut down at Sydenham. 'Isn't it one stinkin' coul day, and am I stinkin' well starvin' from standin' at points duty till my stinkin' feet were so frizz they were nearly stuck to the stinkin' puddles on the stinkin' cobblestones. An' just as I was thinkin' of nippin' 'round the stinkin' corner to yon wee stinkin' widow woman, till have a cup of stinkin' char, then who do you think stinkin' well hoves into stinkin' sight but the stinkin' Rajah hisself [a nickname for a most feared sergeant on the police force], so I just had to put such stinkin' thoughts of comfort out of my stinkin' head and git back till my stinkin' post.'"

Such long spiels of invective would make Dorothy and me curl up and roll with delight on the carpet, and Daddy would beam upon us, well pleased at amusing his wee daughters so easily.

Time passed, and the year I turned 19, our father died. As is usual in Ireland, "the remains," as we fondly call the dead body, was laid out in the back bedroom, and my sister and I were kept busy answering doorbells, pouring strong tea, and handing 'round ham sandwiches and sympathy.

The house was full of grieving relatives and friends, talking of everything from what favorite won at the 3:30 race to the fine character of the "dear departed"—when once again the doorbell's shaky whirr was heard. I hurried to answer, smoothing down my grey woolen dress and adjusting my features to those of bereavement as I opened the door.

On the step stood a little man with white hair and a devout face. He wore an overlong raincoat and turned a stained gray paddy hat between red, roughened hands. I bowed slightly in greeting, and the man moved hesitantly forward, saying, "You won't have heard of me, Miss Kerr, but I used to work with your father during the war. My name is William Dynes."

I looked at him. I had an overwhelming desire to shriek, "Welcome, Stinker Dynes, center of long tirades of fatherly monologues, welcome and a thousand times welcome!" But instead I placed my young hand in his old one and said, "We are pleased that you have come to visit us on this sad occasion. Would you care to view the remains?"

Sedately we climbed the stairs.

Maggi Kerr Peirce of Fairhaven, Massachusetts, was born in Belfast, Ireland, but has lived in the United States since 1964. A popular folk performer since the late 1970s, Peirce captivates audiences with her personal reminiscences and her carefully researched songs and rhymes of Ulster.

ORANGE CHEEKS

Jay O'Callahan

One summer night when my son Ted was about 9 years old, I went in to tell him a bedtime story. Ted said, "Tell about when you were bad, Daddy." And out came "Orange Cheeks." After I told him the story, I went into my bedroom and told my wife I'd better record that one. I did, and I'm glad. It brings back the mysteries of Grandmother and her wonderful wrinkles.

Willie was 6 years old, and he lived in the country. One day the phone rang, and Willie picked it up. He had a habit of breathing into the phone instead of talking.

"Hello, Willie," his grandmother's voice said to the breathing.

"How'd you know it was me?"

"I just knew, Willie. Willie, I want you to spend the night."

"Oh, Grandma! I'll get Mama!"

His mother took the phone, talked a while, and hung up.

"Willie," his mother said, "I never let you spend the night at your grandmother's because you get in trouble."

"I won't get in trouble," Willie burbled. He shone with excitement, so his mother said quietly, seriously, "I don't want to get a call tonight and have to drive 30 miles to pick you up."

"No troubllllle," he said.

"Your grandmother can be difficult late in the day," she went on. "She can be a bit of a grump."

"I'll be good. I promise."

"If there's any trouble, you won't go overnight again for a year. Go up and pack your bag."

Willie ran upstairs and put six T-shirts and a toothbrush in his bag.

They drove all the way into Cambridge. Willie loved Cambridge because all the houses were squeezed together. They drove around Harvard Yard and down Trowbridge Street and took a left on Leonard Avenue. The houses were all wooden triple-deckers, and his grandmother lived at Number 9. They parked, and Willie ran up the outside stairs, pushed the outside door open, and pressed the buzzer inside.

Zzzzzttt! The door wouldn't open until his grandmother pressed another buzzer from the inside. It made a click, then the door unlocked. It was magic. Willie pushed the door in and stood at the bottom of the stairs. The stairs were narrow and dark and filled with the wonderful smells of his grandmother's house. He could have spent the whole weekend right there, but his grandmother was standing at the head of the stairs, calling him.

"Come on up, Willie."

"Here I come, Grandmaaaaa."

He rushed up to the top, and his grandmother leaned down for a hug. He kissed her on those wrinkled, crinkled cheeks. He loved those cheeks but never said anything about them.

"You'll be in the guest room upstairs," his grandmother said. "There's a prize up there for you."

"Thank you, Grandmaaaaa," he said, hurrying up the stairs. His mother's voice caught up with him: "You remember what I said, Willie."

"Don't worry. No troubllllle."

Willie loved the guest room because his grandmother had done something wonderful. She had pasted six large silver stars to the ceiling. He loved those.

The prize lay on the table. Two pieces of orange paper, a small pair of scissors, glue, and a sharp pencil. Willie took the scissors and cut two circles from the paper and put glue on the back of the circles. He pasted the circles to his cheeks. Now he had orange cheeks.

Looking out the window, he saw his mother driving off. "Goodbye, Mamaaaaa," he said with a victorious grin.

He ran downstairs, and his grandmother said just the right thing: "Wonderful cheeks."

"Thank you, Grandmaaaaa," he said, jouncing his shoulders.

"We'll have tea in the dining room, but first I'll hang out wash, and you'll go to Mr. Murchison's. You know him."

"The fruit man."

"Yes. He's right next door. He's expecting you. Get four pounds of bananas. Here's a dollar. Do a good job."

Willie went down the dark narrow stairs, the secret stairs, and on outside to the fruit store. It was an old-fashioned fruit store. Dark. The floor was dark and wooden and oily. Mr. Murchison stood there. He was older than the bananas. And he was curved like the bananas. "Hello, Willie," he said in a long dark voice. "Your grandmother told me you were coming. Nice to see you again." He reached to the top of the banana rack. "I've got four pounds of bananas for you."

Willie shook his head back and forth. "I don't want those."

"What's the trouble?" Mr. Murchison asked.

"They're rotten."

"They're not rotten," mustachioed Murchison insisted, laughing. "They're ripe. Best way to have 'em."

"I want the yellow ones," Willie said.

Mr. Murchison replaced the bananas and took yellow ones from the rack. "Someday you'll know better," he growled.

"Think I know better now," Willie replied.

Mr. Murchison seemed to be chewing something distasteful. "I like your cheeks," he finally grunted.

Willie looked up. "I like your cheeks too."

"Arrrrr."

Willie took the bananas to the back yard, where his grandmother was hanging clothes on the line. "Good for you, Willie. You're a regular businessman. You go up and play till I finish, and we'll have tea."

Willie thought he was a businessman. To him a businessman was someone who made pencil marks on the walls. Secret ones. But they were real. Willie went up and down the back stairway, making small pencil marks. Then he decided to make a secret mark in the dining room.

He pushed a chair against the white wall in the dining room, stood on the chair, reached way up, and started to make a tiny dot. Willie heard something. Terrified, he called, "Grandma!" In his panic he made a scratch mark two feet long on the wall.

"Oh, no! I have to go home now," he cried. He tried to erase it, but that made it worse. He spat on his hands and tried to wipe the mark off. Now it was all over the wall. It was horrible. Now he was in trouble.

He jumped off the chair and ran to the window. His grandmother was hanging the last few socks. He had to do something, or he'd have to go home. Willie opened the drawer in the pantry and saw a hammer and two nails. He took them and went in the dining room. He took the dining-room tablecloth off the table and stood on the chair. He nailed the tablecloth to the wall. Now you couldn't see the scratch mark, but you could see the dining-room tablecloth.

His grandmother made the tea and put everything on a tray.

"Come on, Willie. We'll have tea in the dining room."

His head seemed to be sinking into his shoulders. "Let's have tea here," he said.

"We always have tea in the dining room," she said and went into the dining room alone.

"Willie, the dining-room tablecloth is not on the table," she said in a voice slightly changed. A voice that had new information. "The dining-room tablecloth is nailed to the wall."

After a silence Willie said, "Which wall?"

"You come in and see which wall."

Willie came slowly in. His head sank further into his shoulders. "Oh, that wall," Willie said. "I nailed it to that wall."

Suddenly, he began to shake. His whole body trembled, and he burst out crying. "Now I have to go home." He was crying so hard the tears ran down onto his paper orange cheeks. He began to rub the cheeks, and the paper was tearing and shredding. That overwhelmed his grandmother. "Willie!" she said, rushing over, kneeling down, holding him. She was crying now, and her tears were falling onto his paper orange cheeks. She held him until she could get hold of herself, then breathed deeply, saying, "Willie, look at the two of us. This is absurd. Everything's all right."

"No, it isn't," Willie sobbed. "Now I have to go home. I can't come for a whole year."

"You don't have to go home," she said, standing. "It's perfectly all right."

"No, it isn't," Willie persisted. "Mama says late in the day you're a grump."

His grandmother's eyes seemed to open rather wide. "Hmm. She does, does she?" His grandmother pursed her lips in thought. "Well, I'll tell you this, Willie—your mother's no prize either."

They sat down at the table. "Now we'll have tea, and then we'll take care of the wall. How many sugars, Willie?"

"Five."

"One," she corrected.

The tea seemed to calm his whole body.

"Now, your mother won't know about this," she said with assurance. "It's our secret."

"She'll know," Willie pouted. "She always knows."

"She's my daughter. She won't know."

His grandmother took the hammer and pulled out the nails. She put the tablecloth on the table, saying, "I'll sew the holes up another time, but your mother won't know. I'll put a bowl of fruit over one hole and flowers over the other." His grandmother put putty in the holes in the wall, and that afternoon she and Willie painted over the scratch mark.

In three hours the paint was dry, and the mark was gone. "Now your mother won't know about this," she said with assurance. "It's our secret."

"She'll know," Willie pouted. "She always knows."

"She's my daughter. She won't know."

"She's my mother. She'll know," Willie grumped.

Willie was scared to death as his mother came up the dark secret stairs the next morning. The three of them would have tea before leaving.

They sat at the dining table drinking tea. Willie was quiet as long as he could be. Finally, he looked at his mother and said, "Don't pick the bowl of fruit up."

"Why would I pick the bowl of fruit up?" she asked.

An extraordinary look of total innocence filled his face. "I don't knooooow."

Tea continued, and Willie kept staring at the wall.

"What are you staring at?" his mother asked.

"The wall," Willie replied. "It's a nice wall."

"Ah!" his mother said. "There was trouble, just like I said. What happened?"

Defeated, Willie said, "Tell the trouble, Grandma."

"Well, there was trouble," his grandmother said kindly. "The trouble was, we didn't have enough time. Is that what you mean, Willie?"

"That's what I mean," he said, bouncing.

A few minutes later his grandmother stooped over at the top of the stairs, and Willie kissed her on those wrinkled, crinkled cheeks. And then he and his mother went down the dark narrow stairway with the wonderful smells. His mother didn't know what had happened. It was a secret.

When he got home, Willie ran up to his room, unzipped his bag, and took out the orange paper. He cut two circles and put them in an envelope with a note saying, "Dear Grandma, Here's orange cheeks for you. Love, Willie."

Jay O'Callahan has performed his one-man theatrical productions at Lincoln Center and the Library of Congress and throughout the country. As a teenager, he began telling stories to his younger brother and sister. O'Callahan became a professional teller in 1975 and continues to be at the vanguard of the storytelling movement. He lives in Marshfield, Massachusetts.

THE SEAL SKIN

Lynn Rubright

First collected in Iceland by Jon Gudmundsson the Learned in 1641, this story has an unsettling contemporary message. Suggesting that man is connected to nature in ways many of us have forgotten, the tale also poignantly illustrates the far-reaching consequences our choices can have.

Gunnar had lived in the hut nestled between two craggy cliffs near Myrdal by the Sea for as long as anyone could remember. It was where he was born and raised. Now he lived there alone.

Over the years Gunnar noticed that a strange occurrence took place now and again near the rocky shoreline. It took him many years to discover that it only happened on Midsummer's Eve.

The first time he remembered stopping to listen to the music, he was just a boy. His mother had called to him: "Gunnar, even though the sun is shining, it is late. Come inside now."

"But Mother, I am listening to the music. Come here, and you will hear it too."

"Nonsense, child, it is only the wind. Come, it is time for bed."

The next day Gunnar scrambled up the rocky cliff overlooking the sea and listened. But only the wind howled. "Mother was right; it is nothing."

Years passed before he heard it again. This time he was in his small skiff, pulling in fishing lines. Again it was Midsummer's Eve, and although the hour was late, the Icelandic night was bright as day. By the time Gunnar came ashore, brought in the fish, and untangled his nets, he was weary.

Icelandic summer days and nights flow into one another, and a few hours' sleep are usually enough. It is not uncommon to work 20 hours a day. But then one must rest too.

Gunnar told himself, "I will go listen to the music a little later." But he fell asleep, and when he returned to listen, all he heard was the wind. "Perhaps I was imagining it again," he said.

He went along the shore, seeing nothing except a dark opening to what might be a cave. Gunnar climbed up the rocks and looked inside. It was dark and still—and yet there was a smell of fish. No, it smelled more of seal skins. Gunnar went inside, and there he found ashes still warm from a fire.

When he looked around, he saw no one was there, but music seemed to echo against the rock walls of the cave. "Someone was singing here last night, I'm sure."

As Gunnar came out of the cave, he looked out to sea and noticed seals swimming and playing in the waves. "That is strange," Gunnar murmured. "I have never noticed seals in this place before, swimming so close to shore."

Every day that summer Gunnar walked the shore, listening amid the often howling gales of the wind. He came each day, in all kinds of weather, often climbing to the cave. But he never saw anything unusual, nor did he hear the music.

The winter was long and hard, and for many months Gunnar forgot about the music of last Midsummer's Eve. Then the days grew longer, and as summer approached, he remembered.

Again Gunnar began walking the shore near the cave. He saw and heard nothing unusual. But on the day of Midsummer's Eve Gunnar stayed away. Not until close to midnight did he stealthily make his way over the rocks near the cave. Then he sat well hidden but close enough to hear. There it was: music and laughter and voices. Gunnar peeked over the rock and saw on the shore seal skins, dozens of them, lying on the ground.

Then he remembered something his grandmother had told him when he was very small: "Little Gunnar, be gentle with the seals, my child. They are so like us. Look at their bones when you have taken their skins and meat—you will find them almost human in their shape. And their eyes, little Gunnar, round and black, cry tears when they are sad. You know, some say soldiers from Pharaoh's army were turned into seals when the Red Sea closed over them after Moses led the children of Israel through the walls of water. As a gift of grace, some say, they are allowed to come onto shore once a year, shed their skins, and dance and sing until dawn. But of course, no one has ever seen or heard them, so no one knows if this is true."

As Gunnar listened to the music, he got an idea. Carefully he slid down among the rocks and made his way to where the seal skins lay on the shore. He reached out and grabbed one. Tucking it under his tunic, he ran back to his hut. Gunnar put the skin into a little wooden box and locked it with a small brass key. Then he lit the fire in the stove and waited. Smoking his pipe by the fire, Gunnar sat until the early morning light became brighter. Of course, on Midsummer's Eve night it never gets completely dark.

Early in the morning Gunnar went again near the shore by the cave, staying well hidden among the rocks. When he looked, he saw a beautiful girl sitting on a rock, weeping. All the seal skins were gone. *Grandmother's story is true*, thought Gunnar. *There are seal people who come from the sea to sing and dance on Midsummer's Eve. How beautiful this seal woman is.* Gunnar felt pity and love for her.

He ran back to his hut, grabbed a wool blanket, and hurried back to where the girl was sitting, shivering without clothes. Gunnar called to her gently. Slowly he walked toward her, unfolding the blanket. She was frightened, but she allowed herself to be wrapped in the warm wool.

Gunnar took her hand and gently led her back to his hut. The girl was friendly toward Gunnar. When she had learned to speak, she often told him of losing her seal skin when the Midsummer celebration was over and how her family had returned to the sea without her. But Gunnar never talked of the seal skin or where he had hidden it.

Often on Midsummer's Eve, Hildar, for that is what Gunnar called her, would beg to return to the cave to listen to the music. But Gunnar always said she must not go, for it would only cause her grief. Without her seal skin, she could never be part of her seal family again. Great tears would roll down her cheeks at the thought of her seal family. Often she would hum a sad melody—but she would never sing the words.

As time passed, Hildar gave birth to many children—seven in all. She loved them very much, but she never was comfortable with other people in the village. Only with Gunnar did she feel safe. And with her children.

Gunnar gave Hildar everything she wanted or needed, but often he would say, when she asked what was in the little wooden chest, "Oh, nothing of importance to you. Only my inheritance. That is why I always keep it locked. It is of no interest to anyone but me." But Hildar noticed that Gunnar always kept the key tucked in his shirt pocket.

One Christmas Eve, Gunnar and the children prepared to go to church. Hildar wasn't feeling well and decided to remain home to tend the fire, as the night was bitter cold, with a howling wind. After her husband and children had gone, Hildar took Gunnar's shirt from the peg and discovered the little brass key. For a long while she held it in her hand and looked at the wooden box. Then she gave in to curiosity.

Kneeling down, Hildar unlocked the box, and when she opened the lid, she was startled to see inside, neatly folded, her own seal skin. She knew if she ever touched it, she would not be able to resist the temptation to try it on.

Hildar sat with the key in her hand, looking at the seal skin. All the memories of her life under the sea came back to her. She remembered too the seven beautiful seal children she had left behind, and a great longing filled her heart. Hildar knelt down and touched the seal skin. She was overcome with a desire to put it on. As she did, she became a seal once again. Out the door she went, making her way down to the water's edge. Some say that as she slipped into the water, she sang the words to her song,

Woe is me! Woe is me!

I have seven children on the land
And seven in the sea.

When Gunnar and the children returned to the hut, the door was open, and in the shadow of the fire's smoldering embers they saw that the little forbidden box had been opened and was empty. And their mother was gone. Gunnar knelt down and wept, for he knew what had happened.

Never did Hildar return to Gunnar and her children. Nor did the seals ever return at Midsummer to the cave at Myrdal to dance and sing. But often Gunnar noticed one seal swimming about his boat. When she looked up at him, tears seemed to flow from her beautiful eyes. The seal would often guide Gunnar's boat to rich fishing grounds, and his catches became very good.

And when the children were playing on the beach, they noticed that a seal often flipped fishes and pretty shells to them. But as their mother she never returned to them.

Lynn Rubright, the co-founder of the annual St. Louis Storytelling Festival, developed Project Tell—a federally funded storytelling-in-education program. Rubright creates operas and historic interpretive dramas and performs worldwide as an inspirational keynote speaker. She lives in Kirkwood, Missouri.

WICKED JOHN AND THE DEVIL

Jackie Torrence

Many years ago there was a man named John who lived in the mountains of North Carolina. Ever'body called him Wicked John 'cause that's just what he was—one of the wickedest men you'll ever lay eyes on. Old John was mean and stingy and just downright hateful. He was so mean, even his wife was scared of him. Wicked John was a blacksmith by trade, and folks did say that he was a mighty, mighty fine blacksmith.

Ever' mornin' Wicked John would get up and yell down to his wife, "Woman, is my breakfast ready?"

And his wife would say, "Yes, Wicked John," and then she'd run off into the closet and lock herself in.

Old Wicked John would stomp down the stairs and over to the table and eat just as quickly as he could. When he finished, he would get up and walk down the road to his blacksmith shop. As he stood in front of the locked door, he would pull a set of keys from his pocket, open the door, prop it open, go into the shop, and prepare his work for the day.

One day as Wicked John unlocked the door and propped it open, he all of a sudden saw a bright and shining glow in the back of the shop. That made Wicked John a little angry, so he yelled, "Who's that back there in my shop?"

All of a sudden the light cleared, and standing there was an angel, and the angel said, "Good mornin', Wicked John."

Wicked John said, "Who are you?"

The angel said, "Wicked John, I have come to give you three wishes."

"Wishes?" said Wicked John. "Wishes? I don't want your wishes. Get out of my shop."

"Well," said the angel, "we've been watchin' you, and we know that you're an awfully unkind man, and if you don't take these wishes, you won't go to heaven when you die."

"Listen here," said Wicked John. "If you don't get out right now . . . just look at you, droppin' them feathers all over my shop. Get on out of here."

When I was a child, my elementary school librarian, Miss Corrine Thomas, would gather the children around her and read to them from a book. But as she read, she never turned the pages. I soon learned that Miss Thomas wasn't really reading the tale: she was telling it. This is my version of one of the stories Miss Thomas told us.

But the angel said, "I can't leave until you take the wishes."

"Wishes?" said Wicked John. "All right. I'll take the wishes. Now let me see. Wishes . . . Wishes . . . I know exactly what I want to wish for. Do you see that hammer over there? Well, that hammer is what I work with every day, and every time I start to work in my blacksmith shop, men come up from town and git to messin' and feelin' and touchin' my work, especially my hammer. Well, I want to put on that hammer a wish that if anybody touches it, that hammer sticks to 'em, and they won't be able to turn it loose until I say so."

The angel said, "What an awful wish."

Wicked John said, "But that's my wish. Do I git it or don't I?"

"So be it," the angel said. "You have your first wish. But be very careful. For you see, you have only two more."

"Well," said Wicked John, "I've got me another wish. Every time I finish work here in my blacksmith shop, I go home in the afternoon to git a chance to sit on my porch a spell before suppertime. Well, somebody's always a-sittin' in my favorite chair. I wish that anybody I catch sittin' in my chair won't be able to git outa it till I say so."

The angel said, "Good heavens. That's an awful wish."

"It's my wish. Do I git it or don't I?"

"Oh yes," said the angel. "So be it. You have one more wish."

"Huh . . . Huh . . . Huh . . . Well, I'll tell ya," said Wicked John. "I make plenty of money here in this blacksmith shop, and I put it all right here in my pocketbook, and then I put my pocketbook in my pocket. When I go home, I put my pocketbook on the dresser. My wife drags my money out of my pocketbook and says she's got to buy this and she's got to buy that. I never can keep my money. I want to wish that any money I put in my pocketbook won't be able to come out 'less I say so or until I'm dead."

"Oh," the angel said. "What an awful wish."

"It's mine. Now, do I git it or don't I?"

The angel said, "So be it."

And the angel disappeared.

Wicked John lived on, and he got meaner and meaner and meaner. One day he walked down to the blacksmith shop, unlocked the door, and propped it open, and sure enough, he saw a bright and shining glow. Wicked John said, "Who's that back there in my shop?"

The light cleared away, and there standing before Wicked John was the devil himself. Wicked John said, "How do you do? What do you want?"

And the devil cackled and said, "I want *you*."

"Please," Wicked John said. "Can't I finish my work?"

The devil said, "No, you can't. I'm ready to take you now."

"But I've got to work," said Wicked John. "You see, I'm a man that's known for gittin' all of his work done, and I've got to keep on workin'."

The devil said, "You oughta thought about that a hundred years ago when you was bein' mean. I'm goin' to take you away from here. You's makin' my name somethin' awful here on earth."

Wicked John said, "All right. I know I've got to go with you, so if you'll just let me finish my work, I'll go easily."

The devil laughed and said, "Hurry up."

Well, Wicked John went to work, but he worked slower and slower and slower, and soon the devil got madder and madder and madder, and after a while the devil said, "Listen here. I'm ready to go."

Wicked John said, "Well, if you want me to go, maybe you can help me work."

"All right," the devil said. "What do you want me to do?"

Wicked John said, "You can help me do some hammerin'."

The devil said, "Where's the hammer?"

Wicked John said, "Right over there on the table."

The devil walked over and took a look at the hammer. Well, the hammer was big, and it looked heavy, so the devil thought he oughta pick it up with both hands, and he did. He tried to hand it to Wicked John, but the hammer didn't move. It just stuck to the ol' devil.

"Turn me loose," said the devil. "Turn me loose."

Wicked John asked, "Havin' a little problem there?"

The devil said, "You know I am. You know I am. You git me offa this hammer."

Wicked John said, "I'll be glad to, but you've got to make a little bargain with me."

The devil said, "Bargain? Bargain? I don't bargain with the likes of you."

Wicked John said, "Well, you can stay on that hammer then."

"All right," said the devil. "What kind of bargain do you want me to make with you?"

Wicked John said, "I want you to go away, and don't come back botherin' me no more."

The devil said, "I can't do that. I done promised myself that I's goin' to take you offa this earth, and your soul's goin' to be mine. I'm stuck to ya. But I'll tell you what. I'll go away for 20 years, and at the end of 20 years, I'm comin' back to git you, and I ain't pickin' up no hammers neither."

Wicked John said, "Is that the best you can do?"

The devil said, "You can take it or leave it."

"Well," said Wicked John. "All right. Drop the hammer."

The devil dropped the hammer from his hands, lifted himself up into the air, turned around 15 times, and took off.

Wicked John lived on, and he got meaner and meaner and meaner. He got so mean that his wife hardly ever came out of the closet. Twenty years went by, and Wicked John retired from the blacksmith shop. He went home, and every day he'd sit in his rockin' chair on his front porch and rock. Wicked John was an old man, and he couldn't see too good. He was too stubborn to buy 'im a set of glasses, so he just sat there and rocked.

One mornin' he was lookin' down the road, and he couldn't see who was comin'. All he saw was a shadow. But he could hear the ol' devil's cackle, and Wicked John knew right then and there who it was. Well, that shadow came to the house, put his foot up on the porch, and said, "Howdy, Johnny."

And Wicked John said, "Devil, it must be you."

The devil said, "Yeah, it's me. Now come on. Let's go. Twenty years is up."

"Oh," Wicked John said, "I know 20 years is up, and I might as well go with ya. But I'm an old man, and it's gon' take me a while to pack my clothes."

The devil said, "Pack your clothes? You don't need no clothes. Just get you some short-sleeve shirts, and let's go."

"All right," Wicked John said. "But it's gon' take me a little while to find them short-sleeve shirts. I don't see so good. While I'm gone, why don't you rest here in my rockin' chair, and I'll come back when I git my shirts all packed."

The devil said, "Hurry up."

Wicked John went in and stayed and stayed and stayed. After a while the devil got tired of waitin', so he got up and walked over to the door. But when he got up, the chair got up with 'im. The devil was stuck to the chair, and he screamed, "Git me outa here." He lifted 'imself offa the ground and ripped the front porch and roof right offa the house. Old Wicked John stuck his head out the front door and said, "Havin' a little problem there?"

The devil said, "You know I am. You git me outa here."

"All right," said Wicked John. "I'll git you outa there, but you've got to make a little bargain with me."

The devil said, "There you go again. Bargains, bargains. I done told ya. I don't bargain with the likes of you."

"Well," said Wicked John, "you can just take me on then, but that chair will go with you."

"All right," said the devil. "I know what you want. You want me to go away again, but you see, you ain't got 20 years left. I'll go away this time for five years, but at the end of them five years, I'm comin' back, and I ain't pickin' up no hammers, and I ain't sittin' in no chairs."

Wicked John said, "Is that the best you can do?"

The devil said, "Take it or leave it."

"All right," said Wicked John. "Drop the chair."

And the devil dropped the chair, lifted into the air, turned around 20 times, and took off.

Wicked John lived on, and he got meaner and meaner and meaner. One day five years later Wicked John was takin' his mornin' walk. The old man's eyesight had completely gone. He was so blind he had to walk with two canes. He was goin' down the road, walkin' along, when somebody stopped right beside 'im. He couldn't see who it was, but he could hear 'im cackle, and he could smell brimstone, so right away he knew.

Wicked John said, "Mornin', Devil. I know that's you."

The devil laughed. "You're goin' in the right direction, Johnny. Keep a-movin'."

"I know I can't fight you no longer," said Wicked John. "I'll just keep a-goin' like I am."

The devil and Wicked John walked down the road, and the devil was so proud and happy that he finally had Wicked John's soul that he commenced to kickin' dust into Wicked John's face, and Wicked John began coughin'.

The devil said, "What's wrong with you?"

Wicked John said, "Look at ya. You're kickin' that dust and dirt into my face, and it's gittin' my throat all dry. I need to git the dust outa my throat so I can go on."

The devil said, "Well, git it out."

But Wicked John said, "I need me a cold drink."

The devil said, "Where do you expect to git it?"

"I ain't sure where we are," said Wicked John. "You know, I don't see so good, but is that a store across the road?"

The devil said, "Yeah, it is."

"I'll tell you what," Wicked John said. "I'll go over there and git me a cold drink, and when I git the dust and dirt outa my throat, I'll be able to go right on home with ya."

The devil said, "Well, hurry up."

So Wicked John started across the road. But all at once he stopped right in his tracks, turned around, and faced the devil. "Listen here," he said. "I was comin' outa my house so fast this mornin' that I forgot to pick up my money and put it in my pocketbook. I ain't got no money. Would you loan me a quarter?"

The devil just cackled and said, "I ain't got no quarter."

"Oh," said Wicked John, "what am I gonna do?" Then he thought for a minute. "I'll tell you what," said Wicked John. "They tell me that you can turn yourself into any shape or form that you want."

The devil laughed and said, "That's right."

Wicked John said, "Well, why don't you turn yourself into a quarter and jump up here in my hand? I'll put you in my pocketbook, go into the store, and git myself a cold drink. Then you can turn yourself into a gnat and fly on back out here, and we can just go on home."

The devil said, "That's a good idea. I should've thought of that one myself."

With that, he leaped up into the air, turned around 25 times, and fell back into Wicked John's hand as a quarter. Wicked John opened his pocketbook, dropped in the quarter, closed the pocketbook, laughed to himself, and went on back home.

Everything would have been fine, but Wicked John was an old man and didn't live long. Within six months he died in his sleep one night. All the neighbors came to see 'im, and somebody spied Wicked John's pocketbook there on the dresser and wanted to know how much money the old man had saved up. One of the neighbors opened John's pocket-book, and out flew the devil. They tell me he's been flyin' 'round ever since.

Jackie Torrence began telling stories in 1976 at a North Carolina public library. Since then her renditions of Br'er Rabbit stories and mountain legends have become synonymous with the best in American storytelling. She lives in Salisbury, North Carolina.

Lincoln's Famous Beard

Lucille and Bren Breneman

It was an October evening in 1860 in the town of Westfield, New York. Grace Bedell, an 11-year-old girl, was in her room, looking at a picture that her father had just given her. It was not a drawing or a painting, yet she could see every hair on Lincoln's head and all the details of his clothing.

Her lamp threw shadows about his face and covered the hollow cheeks. *Whiskers!* she thought.

"How becoming it would be," she said to herself. "Somebody should tell him. All the ladies like whiskers. They would tell their husbands to vote for him, and he would become president. I must tell him!"

She reached for a pen and began to write the following letter:

Mr. Abraham Lincoln

Dear Sir:
I am a little girl, 11 years old, but I want you to be president of the United States very much. So I hope you won't think me very bold to write to such a great man as you are.

Have you a little girl about as large as I am? If so, give her my love and tell her to write me if you cannot answer this letter. I have four brothers, and some of them will vote for you. If you will let your whiskers grow, I will try to get the others to vote for you. You would look a good deal better, for your face is so thin. All the ladies like whiskers, and they would ask their husbands to vote for you. Then you would become president.

Grace Bedell

At that time about 50 letters a day arrived at the Lincoln campaign headquarters. Lincoln saw only those from friends and very important

When I [Lucille] teach a storytelling class, one of the most rewarding assignments is asking the students to write a story based on fact. I was surprised and pleased when Hideko Asou, a Japanese student at the University of Hawaii, chose one of America's greatest presidents as her subject. With a few changes, here is her story.

people. His two secretaries, John Nicolay and John Hay, considered all other mail unimportant and usually did not give it to Lincoln.

Grace's letter was picked up by John Hay, and he was intrigued by her original idea. But John Nicolay was not impressed and suggested that Grace's letter be tossed into the wastebasket. The two secretaries began to argue, and neither of them would give in.

Just then Mr. Lincoln walked into the room. Now, Abe Lincoln liked little girls. No little girl's letter should be tossed into the wastebasket. He took the letter and began to read it. Soon a pleased expression came to his face.

A few days later Grace received this letter from Springfield, Illinois:

My dear little Miss:
Your very agreeable letter of October 15th has been received. I regret the necessity of saying that I have no daughters. But I have three sons, one 17, one 9, and one 7 years of age. They, with their mother, constitute my entire family.

As to the whiskers, having never worn any, do you not think people would call it a piece of silly affectation if I were to begin now?

Your very sincere well-wisher,
A. Lincoln

You can imagine the thrill and excitement the young girl felt when she read this letter.

On February 16 the following year, a special train carried the newly elected President Lincoln from Illinois to the White House. The people of Westfield learned that the train would stop briefly at a station near their town. The Bedell family also heard the news, and on that day they took

Grace and went to the station. As they approached, they saw a huge banner, which read HAIL TO THE CHIEF, and the Stars and Stripes flying from the roof of the station.

As Grace looked around at the many strange faces, there was a sudden silence. A thousand people were straining to hear. "Here comes the train!" someone shouted.

Grace raised her eyes as high as she could and saw the top of the black railway engine pass slowly beyond the heads of the people in front of her. Then she saw the top of a flat railway car, and another, and a third with the Stars and Stripes waving from the back of it.

Then she saw a tall black hat a little higher than a lot of other hats— that was all that she could see. Some of the people were shouting, "Speech! Speech!" Grace held her breath. All the people around her were quiet.

"Ladies and gentlemen," she heard, "I have no speech to make, nor do I have the time to make one. I appear before you so that I may see you and you may see me."

Grace was ice-cold. That was Lincoln—that was his voice. He was up there on the platform. She tried hard to see him, but all she could see was the tall black hat.

Lincoln was speaking again. "I have but one question, standing here beside the flag: Will you give me the support a man needs to be president of our country?"

The people threw their hats into the air, waved their arms, and shouted, "We will, Abe, we will!" And then they were quiet again because Lincoln had something else to say.

"I have a little correspondent in this place. She wrote me what I should do to improve my appearance. I want to thank her. If she is present, I would like to speak to her. Her name is Grace Bedell."

Grace's father took her hand and started leading her toward the platform. People made a path for them as they went. Her father lifted her up to the platform, up high, where she saw a pair of huge feet.

Somewhere above her she heard a slow chuckle. "She wrote me that I would look better if I wore whiskers."

Then Grace felt strong hands under her arms. She was lifted high in the air, kissed on both cheeks, and gently set down again.

She forgot all about the people. Grace looked up and laughed happily, for up there on the rugged face, she saw the whiskers.

"You see, Grace, I let them grow just for you."

All Grace could do was stand there and look at this great, tall, wonderful man. She would have been willing to stay there forever. But Lincoln took her hand, and she heard him say, "I hope to see you again sometime, my little friend." Then she knew the moment had to end. Lincoln helped her down the railway steps, and she obediently went back to her proud father.

She heard the train whistle and the noise of the engine as it started on its way again. People waved and cheered after the train until it was far down the tracks, but in her mind Grace heard only three words—three words repeated over and over: "My little friend."

Lucille Breneman and her late husband, Bren, both speech educators, co-wrote Once Upon a Time: A Storytelling Handbook. *Married for more than half a century, the couple performed stories in tandem until Bren's death in 1989. Lucille Breneman is a professor emeritus of the University of Hawaii and now lives in San Diego.*

A Bell for Shorty

Jim May

My father's nickname was Shorty. He wasn't particularly short. But he was the second son born to a farm family of 12, and when Uncle Ben, the oldest, gave him that name, it stuck. All the farmers around Spring Grove, Illinois, had nicknames: Happy Waggoner, Jerky John, Squirrelly Ashe, Skunk Orvis. Given the range of possibilities, I suppose "Shorty" wasn't so bad, and my father never complained.

He was 51 when I was born. My mother was 42. We're a Catholic family, and I was what used to be called "a rhythm baby." My mother always said we Catholics were always thinking about two things: rhythm and bingo. And if the rhythm didn't work, bingo! I was bingo.

Being an afterthought, I was quite a bit younger than my siblings and in fact became the proverbial spoiled "baby of the family." The best thing about being the youngest was the year that I had Dad all to myself. I was 6, and that was before the days of kindergarten in McHenry County. My sisters were in high school. My brother had a job in town. Mom worked at the Woodstock typewriter factory to supplement the milk check, and my dad took care of me every day that whole year.

I went wherever he went. I remember sitting with him high up on the iron seat of the old tractor, the big iron seat with the holes drilled in it for the rain to drain through. I sat half in his lap, and he surrounded me with his arms as he held the steering wheel. Sometimes I'd help him steer. Sometimes I'd watch intently as the ground turned over in a furrow behind the plow, and sometimes I would just daydream while holding onto his arms and enjoying the smell of after-shave and sweat.

In summer we'd often stop under the chokecherry tree that grew along the fence row. I'd climb out onto the tractor and pick the berries. Now, they aren't called chokecherries for nothing. They were bittersweet at best, with a large pit in the center, but we liked them anyway. I especially liked sitting there in the shade with my father, eating something wild that I had picked out of a tree. Dad could always find wild things to eat:

As a teenager in the turbulent 1960s, I became weary of living in a small town and ashamed of my farm roots. But now that I'm a traveling storyteller, it is my memories of growing up in the rural Midwest that audiences respond to with recognition. Storytelling has brought me home.

hickory nuts, asparagus, wild plums.

During those quiet times under the chokecherry tree we'd listen for the sound of the meadowlark calling from the pasture or the bobolink calling on the wing over the alfalfa and clover. Dad could make a whistling sound that he told me was the song of a Bob White quail.

I had never seen or heard one since northern Illinois is at the extreme end of their natural habitat. But years later in Virginia I heard a Bob White whistle from a woodlot one afternoon. I knew the sound immediately. It sounded like Shorty May.

I thought of myself as more than a tag-a-long. I could drive a tractor, in a manner of speaking, by the time I was 5 years old. In late summer the corn stood tall in the field but was still green and sweet. We'd pull the hay wagon down into the field with the tractor, load up some cut cornstalks, and park the wagon in the barnyard for the cows to eat from when they came up the yard at milking time.

My job was to "drive" the tractor while Dad cut the corn. Once we'd reached the cornfield, he'd put the tractor into first gear and then hold the clutch pedal to the floor. Then I'd put my foot down on his big work shoe, and he would slide his foot out from under mine. I kept the clutch depressed by putting all of my weight on it. I had control of that powerful piece of machinery.

Dad would take a wooden-handled corn knife and cut the stalks at their base, swinging the knife in slow, steady arcs. The stalks would lay down, slowly, in the crook of his other arm. When he had a pretty good load of stalks, he'd throw the bundle onto the wagon. As he worked his way across the field row by row, he'd get quite a distance from me and the wagon. At that point he'd holler, "Go!"

I'd start to let up slowly on the clutch. If my foot slipped off the pedal, the tractor would rear onto its big black tires like a red metal stallion, or the engine would die entirely, and I would have failed, for the time being, at my attempt to be a "grown-up" farmer. Usually the clutch would engage slowly, in a jerking sort of way, causing the tractor to lurch forward until the wagon was within easy reach of where Dad stood, holding the bundle of corn. He would holler, "Whoa!" and I'd push the clutch pedal back down. The tractor would stop, with the wagon right alongside where he was cutting.

I was very proud of this maneuver. I knew that my being there on the tractor saved him a lot of time and steps. He was 57 years old, farming 300 acres by himself. Even then I was aware of his age and how hard he worked.

I was also the official "hooker-upper" on the place. Whenever there was a wagon or trailer to hook up to the tractor, I would hold the wagon tongue off the ground while my father backed the tractor into position. When the hole in the metal drawbar of the tractor matched the hole in the wagon or trailer tongue, I'd drop a steel pin through the hole, and we'd be hooked up, ready for work. I knew this hooking job would be almost impossible for my dad to do if he were working alone. I felt sure that he and I were partners in the farming business.

But there were some times when I couldn't come along, couldn't be with him. There was the time I rang the bell.

It was late April, corn-planting time. The McHenry County farmers say you plant your corn "when the oak leaves are the size of a squirrel's ear." It was the morning of a soft spring day—a planting day. I helped Dad hook up the planter and watched him fill it with seed and fertilizer. Then he said, "You'll have to stay home today."

I didn't understand why at the time, and it seemed a terrible injustice. Looking back, I think he may have been afraid to have me sitting with him on the tractor seat. We used an old two-row planter that had been converted from horse-drawn, and a man sitting on the tractor had to reach around and backward to put the planter in gear by hand. The marker arms would have to be lifted and dropped again at the end of each row so that each row of corn seed would be properly spaced for future cultivating and harvesting. With all that movement, a small boy could easily be bumped and could fall under the tractor wheel.

When he was ready to leave for the field that day, he said, "I know you'll be alone, so if there's trouble, ring the bell." The rusty old bell hung from a frame on the roof of a storage shanty attached to our house, and I had never heard it ring. A greasy hemp rope dangled from the bell and was tied off high on the rafters. Dad leaned a ladder against the wall and slowly, steadily climbed up to where he could untie the rope from the boards. I held the ladder. The rope uncoiled and fell, its free end almost touching the ground. He climbed back down and said, "Now this isn't for fun or foolishness, but if there's trouble, ring the bell. I'll hear it ring out in the field and come back in on the tractor."

He left for the field, and the time began to drag on ever-so-slowly. I didn't like being alone. I was afraid someone might come down the driveway. It wasn't only strangers who scared me. I was just plain shy, frightened of even the neighbors. I had a lot of four-legged friends and two-legged friends with feathers, but I wasn't used to being around people. So I thought maybe I'd go into the shanty to kill some time.

The shanty had originally been built for carriages and was much too small for the big cars people had in the '50s. We used it to store odds and ends, bald tires, and a few old license plates nailed to the wall. I liked to go in there because I could usually find some greasy, rusty thing to play with. So it was with a mild sense of adventure that I entered the old dusty building.

When my eyes had adjusted to the darkness, I saw our dog, Bootsie— a yappy, ornery cross between a rat terrier and a Chihuahua—curled up in a dirt hole. And sleeping right next to her was a snake. I thought to myself, *This could be trouble*, and I looked up at the bell.

I liked the idea of ringing it and of Dad's coming in from the field at my beckoning. Then I wouldn't have to wait the long, dreary hour or two till he came back for our noon dinner. So I grabbed the old hemp rope and gave it a pull that literally lifted my feet off the ground.

The low, rich toll of the bell sounded out over the fields. The pigeons flew up off the barn, and the heifers jumped around in the pasture with their tails straight in the air. I guess they had never heard the bell either. I liked the sound so much that I rang it again.

When the sound had drifted away, I heard something else: my father's tractor. Every tractor engine sounded different to me, and this was his, coming in from the field. He had heard the bell.

It wasn't long before a sooty line of exhaust appeared over the corn crib near the barn, and then I saw Dad wheeling the tractor around the corner of the tool shed, really moving. He had the old International "H" tractor in road gear. It was unheard of for him to drive that fast because most of his life he had farmed with horses—big muscular Percherons and Belgians with feet the size of serving platters and withers as high as a man's forehead. He loved those big horses and could do anything with them. But he never really trusted tractors and machinery. On those metal beasts he always drove real slowly. So when I saw how fast he was driving the tractor that day, I thought that maybe I was in trouble.

He braked the tractor, bringing it to a stop right in front of me. When he killed the engine, it got real quiet, like it always does when a big engine shuts off.

"What's the trouble?" he asked.

"There's a snake over there by Bootsie!" I said.

Well, it turned out to be just a garter snake about eight inches long. But I didn't get in trouble. Dad let go with a big sigh, like he was relieved that I was safe and sound. He got off the tractor and walked toward the house. As he passed me, he said I was bugs, which was his way of scolding me, I guess, but he didn't say any more about it.

We had an early meal. He stayed long enough to hear the farm report and listen to the music that came on after the news on the Old Chicago Barn Dance station. He didn't dance, though. Most days when the music came on, he'd do a little fox trot across the linoleum floor. Dad would dance to the radio in his dusty work overalls until it was time to go back to the field. I think he did it to make me laugh. Since he didn't dance that day, I suppose he was angrier with me than he let on. I never rang the bell again.

The following year on the first day of March we sold the farming business and moved into town. Dad said it was because of "the price of milk and the Republican recession." I think the work was getting too hard for him, hard times or no. March 1 is the day that farm leases are up. A tenant family can move then and be settled in time to get the crop in. But this time we moved to town. There would be no cows for him to milk twice a day. We kept a couple of horses that we pastured at a neighbor's and left the rest behind. He woke me up early on the morning of the sale and asked if I wanted to go feed the heifers. He said I should come because it would be the last time. It's the only thing I remember from the sale.

He got a job in town, working at a factory, which must have been hard for him after working outside all those years, but he never said much about it. The second spring in town he got laid off from the factory and was hired to work on a Lipizzan horse farm. That seemed like a gift from God because Dad loved horses. He was hired to supervise the brood mares and the raising of the foals. In the wintertime, when the foals came, I would go to work with him on weekends, especially if a mare was due. Sometimes we'd sit up all night. Over the years we welcomed a lot of slippery, spindly legged foals into the world.

One day while I was at school, he was leading a big stallion across the hay field to a new barn, when the big horse bolted. The stud horse "threw its head" and jerked on the leather lead that Dad was holding. I remember him saying later, "If I would have let go, I would have been all right." Instead he held on and fought the horse. Maybe Dad remembered his "cowboy" days, when he'd wrestled raw young horses and taught them to behave and work the fields.

But he was old now, and the strain brought on a heart attack. He died a short time later.

There were times later in my life when there was trouble, and I ached to pull on the rope, but I didn't have a bell to ring, and he didn't have a tractor to drive in from the field.

This story lay idle for years, like the old bell. But now when I tell the story, it seems to me like pulling on the rope. And when I see in the eyes of others that they hear that bell, or a bell of their own, then I know I've rung it. And when I realize that a small part of the world still hears about Shorty May, the man who taught me to listen to the land and to its people, I can hear the tractor coming too.

Jim May of Woodstock, Illinois, has worked as a farmer, a construction worker, a schoolteacher, and a college counselor. He became a full-time teller in 1985, and in 1989 he won a Chicago Emmy Award for his televised presentation of "A Bell for Shorty."

THE WOODCUTTER'S STORY

Nancy Schimmel

I got to wondering what would happen to a male hero who was suddenly saddled with a baby to take care of. This story is the result. Its ending surprised me. After I told the story a few times, I realized that the youngest prince got on in life the way I do—mostly through serendipity.

Once upon a time there lived a king and a queen who had three sons. When the sons were grown, the king called them together and said, "The time will come when I will no longer wish to be king, and one of you will rule in my stead. Therefore, you must go out, each in turn, to learn about the world. I will give my kingdom to the one who first rescues a woman from mortal danger." He was a traditional sort of king. "Since you are my first-born son," he said to the eldest, "you will have the first chance."

So the eldest prince mounted his fine horse and rode off to seek his fortune, feeling as brave and confident as he looked. He knew exactly what would happen. He would rescue no less than a princess and from something fierce and interesting, like a dragon.

He rode along and rode along, and he came to an old woman standing by the road, holding a frayed rope attached to a sleek and restless nanny-goat. "O prince!" called the old woman, immediately recognizing his station in life, "O prince, please milk my goat, for I cannot milk her."

"Nor can I," said the prince, "for I am a prince, and I was not taught to do such things." The prince rode on and rode on, and he came to a young woman holding a wriggling, yowling baby.

"O prince!" she called, "please feed my baby, for he is hungry as a horse, and I cannot feed him."

"A horse I could feed," replied the prince, "but not a baby, for I am a man, and I was not taught to do such things." The prince rode on and rode on, and he came to an old man standing by the road, holding a large and shiny ax.

"O prince!" called the old man, "please take my ax, for I can no longer swing it. I am a woodcutter for the king, and my house and my tools are yours if you would serve him in my stead."

"I would serve your king, old man," said the prince, "but I cannot stay here in the woods with you. I must learn about the world and rescue some endangered princess. My future and my country's future depend on it."

70

So the eldest prince rode on. Soon he came to a castle, where he put himself in service to a king. He became a valiant knight, fought mighty battles, and killed many men, but somehow he never managed to rescue a princess, or indeed any woman, from mortal danger.

The second prince, still at home, was eager for his chance at the kingdom, but he was puzzled, for he knew that his eldest brother had won fame as a knight yet had failed to win the kingdom. When he asked his father's advice on the matter, the king replied, "There's more to kingship than battles."

Well, the second prince rode out on his fine horse, intending to rescue a princess or at least a fine lady. He took the same road his brother had taken and gave the same answers to the old woman with the goat, the young woman with the baby, and the old man with the ax. But when he arrived at the castle, he remembered his father's advice and put himself in service to the king as a courtier. He learned much of fine manners and smooth speech and something of statecraft and the work of kings. Indeed, he met several princesses and many fine ladies, but not one of them needed rescuing from anything more threatening than boredom.

The last remaining prince was still at home, and being the youngest, he was not so eager to go out into the world. But he knew his father was depending on him to go and seek his fortune, so he curried and fed his horse and asked his father's advice. "Ruling a country requires more than brave deeds and fine manners," said the king. Now, this prince thought to ask his mother's advice as well. "You never know where your fortune might lie," said the queen, "but it helps to look in your own heart."

So the youngest prince rode out on his fine horse, intending to rescue a princess or a fine lady or at least a beautiful maiden. He took the same road his brothers had taken, but when he got out of sight of the castle, he got off his horse and walked awhile, the better to say goodbye to the fields and flowers of home. Then he remounted and rode along and rode along, until he came to the old woman with the goat. When she asked him to milk her goat, the prince said, "As I am a prince, no one ever thought to teach me to milk a goat. However, if you will tell me what to do, I will try."

"Certainly," she said. So the youngest prince dismounted, and under the woman's patient direction he finally managed to milk the fidgety goat. "Thank you," said the old woman, taking the pail of foamy milk. "Now that you can milk the goat, you may have her."

"Whatever would I do with a goat?" cried the prince. But there was no reply, for the old woman had disappeared. The goat looked at the prince expectantly. "Oh, all right," muttered the prince. He took the rope in his hand and mounted his horse. He rode on and rode on, and he came to the young woman with the bawling baby.

"O prince!" she called, "please feed my baby, for I cannot feed him."

"Well," said the prince, glancing sidelong at the goat, "I do seem to have this goat, and I've learned to milk her, but I've never fed a baby."

"There's nothing to it," said the woman. So the prince dismounted and milked the goat, and he and the woman fed the baby. "Now you must burp him," said the woman.

"What?" asked the prince.

"Burp him," said the woman. "Hold him against your shoulder, like so, and pat his back, like this." She spread a napkin on the prince's princely raiment and handed him the baby. "Now that you can feed the baby," she said, "you may have him."

"I can't take this baby," shouted the prince, but it was to no avail, for the young woman had disappeared. The prince sighed, tucked the fat, gurgling baby under his arm, tied the goat's frayed rope to his tastefully bejeweled saddle, and clambered back onto his horse. He rode on and rode on, and he came to the old man with the large and shiny ax. The prince closed his eyes.

"O prince!" called the old man. The prince sighed again and opened his eyes. "O prince, please take my ax, for I can no longer swing it. I am woodcutter for the king, and my house and my tools are yours if you would serve him in my stead."

The prince furrowed his brow. "I would serve your king," he said, "but this seems to be turning out all wrong. I thought I was supposed to learn to be a king and rescue a princess, but instead I seem to have this baby and this goat. I suppose I could use a house and a job as well . . ." The prince scratched his head. "What am I supposed to do?" The old man made no reply but simply offered a gnarled finger to the baby. The prince's horse shifted its weight, the goat bleated, the baby crooned, and off in the woods a bird sang. The prince remembered his mother's words, looked into his heart, and smiled. "I think I will stay here," he said, "and learn to be a woodcutter."

The prince settled easily into his new life. The old woodcutter loved his trade and taught the prince everything he knew. They both had a way with babies, and as the baby grew into a boy, they both delighted in teaching him the names of the woodland flowers and creatures. The boy delighted in everything.

Most of the time the prince was content to be cutting the sweet-smelling wood, keeping house with the old man and the boy, and visiting with the common folk of the nearby farms. His neighbors didn't even think of him as a prince anymore. "The new woodcutter," they called him. Still, he was a prince, and he worried because he wasn't learning about battles or statecraft. He was learning to deal diplomatically with mischievous boys and goats and learning some of the stories the old woodcutter told, but mostly he was learning about hard work and the people who did it.

And then sometimes he would think about his father, the king, waiting patiently for his youngest son to rescue a woman from mortal danger and return to rule the kingdom. The nearest princess was in the castle, and the prince never even drove the wagon there to deliver the wood, for that was still the old man's job. Besides, no one had ever seen a dragon in the neighborhood. A wolf or two, perhaps, but that was no help, for all the beautiful maidens 'round about were sturdy farmhands, and no sensible wolf would have dared attack one of them.

One day as the prince sat musing on his unprincely life, the boy ran into the cottage and pulled himself up on the prince's lap. "You know that girl who comes to visit her grandmother in the house down the path?"

"Mmm," said the prince, gazing into the middle distance.

"Well," continued the boy, "her mother made her a red cape with a red hood, and now all the kids are calling her Little Red Riding Hood. Isn't that funny?"

"That's nice," said the prince, but he wasn't listening. He was thinking that he would have to send word to his father that he would never rescue anyone from anything in this peaceful neighborhood. "You run along and play," he said to the boy, giving him a hug and setting him down. "I'll be along in a bit. I'm thinking about something important." The prince sat for a while longer, frowning, then shrugged his shoulders, got up, and went outside. The boy and the old woodcutter were playing knight and horse. The new woodcutter gazed at them fondly for a moment, then picked up his ax and said, "I'm going to the woods. I'll be back in a while."

It is on the shady path that we will take our leave of the youngest prince. At first he walks slowly, scuffling at leaves, but soon he is whistling, and as he turns the bend that will take him from this story into another one, a ray of sunlight catches his ax, and it seems to wink at us.

Nancy Schimmel of Berkeley, California, began telling tales as a day-camp counselor in 1963 and became a professional teller 12 years later. She specializes in participation stories and is the author of the textbook Just Enough to Make a Story: A Sourcebook for Storytelling.

HOW CAEDMON GOT HIS HYMN

Robert P. Creed

Caedmon was a poor but pious man. He was a simple man with a simple job: taking care of the cows for the great monastery of Whitby. He loved his work, although it was very hard.

Caedmon loved the summer best, when he took the cows up into the hills to pasture. Then he thought about how God had made the warm season as a time for cows and men to eat and grow. God had made the warm season as a time for calves to be born and milk to flow. God had made the warm season for birds to fly back from the south and build their nests. Sometimes Caedmon sat on the hillside and looked at the young moon in the sky and then the first bright wandering stars and watched the calves with their mothers in the pasture. He thought about so many things that his heart felt full.

Caedmon loved the winter too, though his work was harder. As he milked the cows and pitched the hay down from the loft and swept out the cow stalls and carted manure to make the cows comfortable, he thought about how God had made the long winter nights a time for cows and men to rest in.

Sometimes, summer or winter, Caedmon found himself just looking at something beautiful that God had made until he had to tell himself to get back to work. For Caedmon loved his work, but he loved God's work more.

On winter nights after he had finished his work, Caedmon washed himself and then went to the farmhands' dining room for supper. Every night while they ate supper, a monk read to them from the Bible. Caedmon knew and loved the names and the deeds of God's heroes. Sometimes he thought about them as he worked. He thought about them when he sat on the hillside and watched the cows in the summer. He thought about them when he worked in the barn in the winter. They were his friends.

When supper was finished, the monk who had been reading from the Bible would leave the farmhands' dining room. Then one of the farmhands

The great Anglo-Saxon historian Bede tells this story in book IV, chapter 24, of his History of the English Church and People, *which he completed in the early 730s. Although Bede wrote his story in Latin, at least one copy of Caedmon's hymn survives in Old English—the language in which I perform this beautiful poem.*

would take out a tall flat lyre and begin to play it, singing songs about the great heroes of the past. Caedmon knew the names and the deeds of the great heroes of the past, but he didn't love them as he loved God's heroes. When he finished his song, the farmhand would pass the lyre, and the next man too would sing a song about the great heroes of the past.

Caedmon always listened carefully to the songs, but he never sang. He couldn't. At the very thought of singing with the lyre resting on his knee, his mouth dried up, his stomach knotted, and his head throbbed.

It was different in the barn. Caedmon always felt comfortable there. There was no one but the cows to talk to, but there was no one to listen either. So Caedmon had made up a little song he sometimes sang as he milked the cows. His little song had just the rhythm of the songs the farmhands sang to the lyre in the dining room. The little song went like this: "Living Lord beginning made—ah . . . "

The little song pleased Caedmon. When he sang it, he felt very happy. As he did his work, he sang of God's much greater work—the making of the beginning of all things: "Living Lord beginning made—ah . . . "

It was a good song, but Caedmon sang it only to the cows. He was too shy to sing it to his friends. Besides, it wasn't very long. So Caedmon sang his little song to please himself and the cows—and maybe the angels, if they had time to listen.

Day after hard but happy day Caedmon worked, sometimes singing his little song. Night after night Caedmon listened first to the Bible, which he loved most to hear, and then to the other farmhands singing about the great heroes of the past, which he also liked to hear but not as much. Night after night he left the dining room without ever singing aloud even his very little song. No one asked him to sing. And that was just fine with Caedmon.

Things would have been just fine for Caedmon, had they gone on in just this way. But things began to change, although Caedmon didn't notice

76

for a long time. He went about his work as he always did. Sometimes when he was singing his little song softly over and over again, he just didn't hear or see anyone who happened to be close by. If the man spoke, Caedmon would hum and pretend he hadn't been singing and listen carefully to what the man said. Then Caedmon would answer if he had to, very politely. Then he would be quiet till long after the man left. But if someone came into the barn so quietly that Caedmon didn't realize he was close by, Caedmon would go on singing to himself. Some of the men began to steal up and watch Caedmon when they had nothing better to do. They tried to catch him unawares; then they'd tell the others, "Caedmon's in the barn, chewing his cud, just like those cows he feeds!"

Soon the other farmhands began to joke about him behind his back: "I saw ol' Caedmon just now, chewing his cud along with the rest of them. He didn't even see me. Pretty soon we'll have to feed him hay and put *him* into the barn every night."

But Caedmon never noticed. He just went around with a happy smile on his face, singing under his breath, "Living Lord beginning made—ah" while he pitched hay or milked or cleaned out the big barn. He was happy as he worked, and he thought how happy God must have been when He made the beginning and then made everything else and how happy He must be to keep it all going.

So Caedmon became dreamy and smiled all the time, even while he sat in the dining room and ate and listened. He talked less and less to other people and more and more to the cows as he milked them and fed them.

The other farmhands would nudge each other now and then and nod their heads toward him whenever he forgot where he was and mouthed his little song to himself. "You think we ought to try milking him?" one farmhand would say to another and guffaw. But Caedmon never noticed. He was happy with his work and his little whispered song: "Living Lord beginning made—ah . . . "

One night there was a great feast in the farmhands' dining room. After the feast everyone took the lyre on his knee and sang. Caedmon sat back and listened happily for a long time. Then someone said, "Caedmon, it's your turn to sing something for us!"

Caedmon was stunned. The lyre was coming his way! One smiling farmhand was passing it to another, all of them grinning at him. Caedmon got to his feet and began to stumble blindly toward the door. He tried to run, but his feet wouldn't move.

"Dear Father, help!" he prayed. At last he was able to reach the door. "The cows," he croaked. "I've got to look after the cows tonight!"

He'd had a narrow escape. When he got to the cow barn, Caedmon felt better. His breath came back. He bolted the door, took the lamp, and went around to see that every cow was comfortable. That calmed him down. Then he climbed into the loft, made himself a bed from some hay, and settled down for the night. Soon he was fast asleep.

That night Caedmon dreamed that he was sleeping in the barn when a man he'd never seen before came and stood beside him. Although the barn was dark, Caedmon could see the man's face clearly. It was very beautiful. Caedmon felt very peaceful lying there, looking—not at all shyly—at the man's beautiful face.

Then the man spoke. The man knew his name! "Caedmon," he said, "sing me something."

"But I don't know how to sing," Caedmon cried, "That's why I left the feast."

The man looked at him and said firmly, "But you do know how to sing. You shall sing to me!"

"What shall I sing?" Caedmon whispered.

"Sing me creation."

And Caedmon began to sing. He just started and he sang. He didn't think about anything until he stopped singing. This is what he sang:

Now hail we heaven-kingdom's Lord, the
Measurer's might, and His mind's thought, the
Wonder-father's work! Of all things He the
Living Lord beginning made—ah!
First He raised heaven's roof on high, that
Holy Shaper, for sons of men—ah!
Middle-earth then mankind's Lord, the
Living Lord, with all life filled, for
All men's sons, Almighty God, ah!

When Caedmon woke up, he remembered his dream. "But can I really sing the song I sang in my dream?" he said to himself as he climbed down from the loft, washed his hands, and began the morning milking. "Can I remember all the words—the way they went? I don't know; I don't know! Dear Father, please help your very humble servant." He leaned his forehead against the warm flank of the cow as his hands stroked her teats. "How did it go? 'Now hail we heaven-kingdom's Lord . . .' That's it! That's it!" The warm milk flowed from the cow's full bag. And the words came back to him as the milk rose in the pail—all the words of his dream song.

Now Caedmon felt he had to tell his dream to his boss. So he found the reeve who ran the farm and spoke to him. "Can you still sing the dream song?" the reeve asked. Caedmon sang it for him.

"Hmm. I think we'd better go to Lady Hilda and tell her about this dream of yours."

"The Abbess?" Caedmon cried. "The big boss?"

"Yes," said the reeve. "I think she'll want to hear about your dream." So off they went to the great wooden building on the hillside. Caedmon had admired the beautiful building, with its stout timbers rising from the ground and its proud roof sailing high above. But he had never been inside.

Caedmon waited outside. He was trembling. But then he closed his eyes and thought of milking the cows. The reeve came to the great door and beckoned to Caedmon. "The Lady Hilda will see you."

Caedmon entered. Inside, the great building looked even larger. But Caedmon didn't see the tapestries that covered the walls and helped to keep the heat in. He saw only the hard earthen floor and the great fire in the middle of the room. He barely saw the old abbess sitting at a great table. He didn't see her smile at him as he made his way toward her, head bowed, in the reeve's footsteps. The reeve stopped. Caedmon stopped.

"Caedmon," said a gentle voice, "Please tell me your dream, all of it." At first Caedmon was tongue-tied, but soon he was telling his dream to the great lady in the great chair. Soon he got to the song he had sung in his dream and had sung again that morning as he milked the cows. His voice didn't tremble at all as he sang: "Now hail we heaven-kingdom's Lord, the Measurer's might, and His mind's thought . . . . " When he finished, Caedmon bowed his head again. He didn't see how serious the old abbess looked.

Lady Hilda turned to the reeve. "Tell all the brothers and sisters to come here at once." When all of the monks and nuns had gathered together, the abbess told Caedmon to tell them his dream and to sing the dream song. Caedmon did as he was told. When he finished, he opened his eyes and found everyone kneeling.

The abbess got up from her knees and sat down in her great chair. Soon she broke the silence. She turned to the monks and the nuns and called each one by name. "Who was the beautiful man who spoke to Caedmon in his dream?" she asked. And every monk and every nun said the same thing whenever it was his or her turn to speak: "The man was an angel." The old abbess turned to the cowherd.

"Caedmon," she said gently, "do you believe that it was an angel who spoke to you?" Caedmon knelt and bowed his head.

"Yes, My Lady," he said softly.

"Caedmon," said Abbess Hilda, "have you ever sung a song before?"

"Only a little one. It's in my dream song. It's only a little bit of the dream song."

"Can you sing any other songs?"

"I don't know, My Lady."

"Have you ever tried?"

"No, My Lady, I've only sung that little song that's in my dream song."

"Will you try now?"

Caedmon bowed his head and whispered, "What shall I sing, My Lady?"

"Sing God's creation of man!"

"Yes, My Lady, if one of the monks will read the story to me from the Bible again."

Abbess Hilda told a monk to read the story of Adam and Eve to Caedmon.

"Will you sing that story now?" asked Lady Hilda.

"I think I can sing it tomorrow," said Caedmon.

"Why tomorrow?" asked the monk who had read the story to Caedmon.

"Because, sire, I must chew it over . . . "

"Like the clean beast chewing its cud!" said Lady Hilda. "It's true what I've heard about you, Caedmon," she said, smiling. "And tomorrow morning we must draw off the sweet milk of song that has formed itself in your mind.

"Caedmon," she continued, "God has given you a great gift. He has given you the power to turn His Word into song. You are like the good cows you have tended so long and so well. We shall feed you the living Word, and you shall chew your cud until the milk of song flows from your lips into our ears and hearts. And these brothers"—she turned to the monk who had read and to another sitting in the room—"shall take down your words on precious vellum, the sacrifice of little calves that God gives us to keep His Word safe for men and women not yet born."

Caedmon became a brother in the monastery where he listened every day to God's Word. And after he listened, he chewed the Word well. When he was ready, he poured out the song he had made.

Sometimes Caedmon sang the song he had made for monks who sharpened their pens and listened and then dipped their pens in ink and wrote the words down. Sometimes Caedmon sang the song he had made for his brothers and the sisters as they ate. And sometimes Caedmon sang the song he had made for the farmhands who had once laughed at the dreamy, ruminating, simple cowherd to whom God gave the gift of turning His Word into song.

Robert P. Creed, known for his Old English recitations of Beowulf, *is an English professor at the University of Massachusetts at Amherst. Creed has performed and recorded stories since the mid-1970s. He lives in Shutesbury, Massachusetts.*

CINDY ELLIE

Mary Carter Smith

Once upon a time, over in East Baltimore, there lived a happy family: Sam Johnson, his wife, Lula, and their daughter, Ellie. Lula was good and kind—a quiet, church-going woman—but mighty puny and sickly. One day Lula called Ellie to her bedside and said, "Child, Mama ain't feeling so well. One of these days I might leave you."

"Oh, Mama, don't say that," Ellie said, with tears in her eyes. "Don't cry, child," her mama answered. "All of us go sometime, and I'd rather it be me than you. So there are a few things I want to tell you. Always mind your daddy. Stay in church, go to school, and learn that book. Remember what I'm telling you."

"All right, Mama, I'll remember."

One day not long after that, the poor woman just up and died, real peaceful-like and quiet.

Honey, let me tell you, she had a beautiful funeral. Sam sure put her away nice. The Senior Choir turned out full force. The Junior Choir was there. And the Gospel Chorus just sang their hearts out. The church was *crowded*. Folks all on the outside too, with loudspeakers going. Lula's lodge sisters was there in their white dresses and them purple sashes all edged in gold. Ellie was on the front row beside her daddy, just as cute as she could be in a white dress and her hair in a fine bush. Ellie was one purty young black sister, with skin like black velvet.

Child, let me tell you, that poor woman's body wasn't hardly cold before them church sisters was after Sam Johnson like flies after honey! 'Cause he had a good job down Sparrow's Point, with lots of seniority. And they had just paid for one of them big pretty houses on Broadway, with them pretty white marble steps.

That poor man, like so many good men, was weak for a pretty face and big legs and big hips. One hussy, the boldest of 'em all, had a heart as hard as a rock. The milk of human kindness had curdled in her breast. But she did have a pretty face, big legs, and great big hips. Ooh-wee! She

I tell "Cindy Ellie" because of my desire to give urban audiences stories they can relate to. The tale incorporates satire, humor, and African-American traditions and encourages voting, cleanliness, and forgiveness. Written in a mixture of street vernacular and standard English, this story is best read with tongue in cheek.

could put on! Made like she loved Ellie so and was always bringing barbecued ribs, collard greens, cracklin' bread, and jelly layer-cake to Ellie and Sam. Well, that man fell right into her trap. She had him cornered and married before you could say Jackie Robinson.

Then bless my soul. You ain't never seen such a change in nobody. First off, that woman went down to South Car'lina to get her two big-footed ugly gals that her mama'd been keeping. Brought them back to Baltimore, put poor Ellie out of her pretty room with the canopied bed, and let her ugly gals sleep in that pretty room. Made poor little Ellie sleep on a pallet in the cellar.

Now, Ellie's mama had been wise. When everybody else was converting their furnaces to oil and gas, she said, "Uh uh. One day they gon' be hard to get." She had kept her coal furnace. Poor little Ellie had to do all the cooking, cleaning, washing, and ironing. She had to scrub them marble steps twice a day too and wait on them ugly gals hand and foot. Not only that, but in the winter she had to keep the fire going and clean out the ashes and cinders. So they got to calling her Cindy Ellie.

Tell you the truth, I believe that woman had put some roots on that man. 'Cause no matter how she mistreated Cindy Ellie, he never said a word—he was just crazy 'bout that big-legged woman.

That November the good white folks, the good Asian folks, and the good black folks all turned out and voted for a good black brother who was running for mayor, and he won the election by a landslide. He was going to have his inauguration ball down at the Convention Center, and so many folks had voted for him that they had to hold it for two nights running. The mayor's son had come home from Harvard to go to the ball.

Oh, them stepsisters was primping and buying designer gowns to go to the ball. Poor Cindy Ellie had to give one of 'em a perm, the other a jheri curl, and both of them facials—not that it helped much. Honey, them gals was ugly from the inside out.

"Cindy Ellie, don't you wish you could go to the ball?" they teased.

"Oh, you're making fun of me," Cindy Ellie said.

So Cindy Ellie's daddy, her stepmother, and them two ugly gals all went to the ball and left poor Cindy Ellie at home. Now, Cindy Ellie had a godmama. She had been her dear mama's best friend, and she still had a key to the house. She came to the house that night, as she often did, to sneak food to poor Cindy Ellie and found the child lying on her hard pallet, just crying her heart out.

"Why are you crying, child?" she asked her.

"Be-because I want to go to the ball."

Now, this godmama had been born with a veil over her face, down in New Orleans. She knew a thing or two about voodoo and hoodoo. Besides that, she had a High John the Conqueror root that she always used for good. The godmama told Cindy Ellie, "Go upstairs to the kitchen, child. Look in the kitchen-cabinet drawer, and bring me the biggest white onion you can find." Cindy Ellie was an obedient child, so she didn't ask why. She just did what her godmama told her to do. Cindy Ellie brought the onion to her godmama. Then the two of them went out in the back yard. The godmama lay that onion on the ground, and then she stepped back and waved that root over it. And right before their eyes that onion turned into a long white Cadillac that parked itself in the back alley.

"Cindy Ellie, go up to the third floor, and bring me that mouse trap." Cindy Ellie brought it down. In its cage were two little black mice. The godmama told Cindy Ellie to open the cage door, and them mice started out. But that godmama waved that root over them, and they turned into two six-foot-tall black chauffeurs dressed in shining white uniforms with fancy white caps. They had on tall black boots, and they was bowing and scraping. "All right, Cindy Ellie, you can go to the ball now."

"But Godmama, look at me. I'm clean, but I'm ragged."

"Don't worry 'bout it," her godmama said. Then she stepped back and waved that root over Cindy Ellie. Her rags turned into a dazzling dress of pink African lace. Her hair was braided into a hundred shining braids, and on the end of each braid were beads of pure gold. Her eyes were beautifully shaded, and her skin shone like polished ebony. On each ear hung five small diamond earrings. On her tiny feet were dainty golden sandals encrusted with dazzling jewels. Cindy Ellie was laid back!

As one of the chauffeurs helped her into the white Cadillac, her godmama told her, "Be sure you leave before midnight, or you'll be as you was. Your Cadillac will turn back into an onion, your chauffeurs into mice, and your clothes into rags." Cindy Ellie promised that she would leave before midnight. And away she went, as happy as could be.

At the ball, not long afterward, the mayor's son heard that a beautiful girl who looked like an African princess had arrived. He came out to see her and said to himself, "This sure is one fine fox." He asked her, "May I escort you into the ballroom?" Cindy Ellie replied in tones soft and low, "I don't mind if you do." He helped her out of her limousine and escorted her into the ballroom and to the head table.

Every eye was on Cindy Ellie. You could have heard a pin drop. Then voices could be heard, whispering, "Gorgeous," "Lovely," "Devastating," "Elegant." Even the mayor himself could not take his eyes off her. His wife agreed that she was indeed a charming young woman. The other ladies were looking at her clothes and wishing their own gowns were half as beautiful as Cindy Ellie's.

Although the table was loaded with sumptuous food, Toussaint, the mayor's son, couldn't eat a bite—he was too busy looking at Cindy Ellie. Then the band started to play, and Cindy Ellie and Toussaint danced as if they had been dancing together all their lives. Cindy Ellie was friendly and courteous to everyone she met. She even sat beside her stepsisters, who had no idea who she was, and invited them to come back the next night. For Toussaint had begged Cindy Ellie to return for the second night of the ball.

Then Cindy Ellie heard the clock strike 11:45. She murmured to
Toussaint, "Really, I must be getting home," and rushed out as fast as she
could go. As soon as she was home, Cindy Ellie called her godmama and
thanked her for such a splendid time. Then the doorbell rang, and she
heard her stepsisters' voices: "Hurry, stupid! Open the door!"

Cindy Ellie came out, yawning and rubbing her eyes as if she'd been
asleep. "Did you have a good time?" she asked. "Oh, it was all right, but
we didn't get to dance with the mayor's son. He danced only with some
new girl nobody had ever seen before. She had on some ol' African
clothes. But on her they did look good. She had the good sense to recognize what quality people we are, and she asked the mayor's son to invite
all of us to come tomorrow night."

"What was her name?" asked Cindy Ellie.

"No one knows. The mayor's son is dying to find out who she is."

Cindy Ellie said, "You don't mean it. Oh, how I wish I could go to the
ball tomorrow night. Lillie, won't you lend me your old blue gown so I can
go too?" The sisters almost split their sides laughing. "You, with your
ragged self, go to the inauguration ball? Wouldn't that be something else!
Of course not. Come and help us get undressed and turn back the covers
on the bed so we can go to sleep."

And the next night, as on the night before, poor little Cindy Ellie was
left behind while the rest of them went to the ball again. Her godmama
came in and heard the child crying again. "Why you crying, child? You
want to go to that ball again?"

"Yes, ma'am."

"I thought so. You've been a good child all your life, and you always
respect your elders. So don't worry. You can go to the ball again. Now dry
your eyes, and get your face together. Look in that kitchen-cabinet drawer,
and bring me the biggest yellow onion you can find." Cindy Ellie came

back with the biggest yellow onion you ever laid eyes on. Then the two of them went out in the back yard. The godmama laid that onion on the ground, and then she stepped back and waved the root over it. And right before their eyes, that onion turned into a solid gold Mercedes-Benz about half a block long and parked itself in the back alley.

"Cindy Ellie, go up on the third floor, and bring me that rat trap," said her godmama. Cindy Ellie brought it down, and in its cage were two big white rats. You see, the family lived so close to Johns Hopkins Hospital that mice and rats from the laboratories up there used to escape and get into the house. They took that cage out in the back yard, and the godmama told Cindy Ellie to open the door. When them rats started out, the godmama stood back and waved that High John the Conqueror root over them, and they turned into two seven-foot-tall white chauffeurs dressed in shining gold uniforms with fancy gold caps. They had on long white boots, and they was bowing and scraping.

"All right, Cindy Ellie, you can go to the ball now."

"But Godmama, look at me. I'm clean, but I'm ragged."

"Don't worry 'bout it," her godmama said. Then she stepped back and waved that root over Cindy Ellie. Her rags turned into a dress made of pure silk kente, the royal cloth from Ghana, and worth thousands of dollars. On her head was a headdress of the rarest taffeta, standing tall and just gorgeous. Her big pretty eyes were beautifully shaded, and her skin was shining like polished ebony. Golden bracelets covered her arms clean up to her shoulders. On each ear hung five small diamond earrings. On her tiny feet were dainty golden sandals encrusted with dazzling jewels. She was cool!

As one of the chauffeurs helped her into that gold Mercedes-Benz, her godmama told her, "Be sure you leave before midnight, or you'll be as you was. That Mercedes-Benz will turn back into an onion, your chauffeurs into rats, and your clothes into rags." Cindy Ellie promised that she would leave before midnight. Away she went, as happy as could be.

As they drove up, Toussaint was waiting for her. She went into the ballroom draped on his arm. Oh, they was having such a good time, laughing and talking and waltzing and boogieing. That poor child forgot all about the time. Then she heard the clock as it began to strike 12. She ran out of there as fast as her legs could carry her—so fast that she ran out of one of her sandals. Toussaint ran behind her, but he couldn't see where she had gone. He picked up the golden sandal.

He asked the security people, "Did you see an African princess run by you?"

"No," they said. "We did see a girl dressed in rags run out of the door. We thought she had stole something. But that chick was gone!"

That night when the family came home from the ball, they told Cindy Ellie, "Something mighty strange happened tonight. As the clock at City Hall began to strike 12, that African princess began to run like crazy. She ran so fast, she ran right out of one of her golden sandals. The mayor's son found it and kept it. He's really upset over that sister."

Child, the next day the mayor's son came on television, came on the radio, and announced to every paper in Baltimore that he would marry the girl whose foot fit that sandal he had picked up. Now, a lot of folks who had supported the mayor lived in the places surrounding Baltimore. So first all them sorority girls and debutantes and folks like that tried to fit their foot in that sandal. Wouldn't fit none of them girls in Columbia, Cockeysville, Randallstown, and all the places like that. Then they went to them rich folks' houses up on Cadillac Row. Wouldn't fit none of them girls neither. Then they went to all them condominiums downtown by the Inner Harbor and them fancy townhouses. Wouldn't fit none of them neither. Finally they come to East Baltimore.

Length and long they came to Broadway and knocked at the Johnsons' residence. The mayor's men came in with that golden sandal on a red velvet pillow. Them two stepsisters tried their best to put on that shoe. They pushed, and they jugged, but their big feet would not get into that shoe. No way, José!

"May I try?" asked Cindy Ellie.

"No, stupid. It's not for the likes of you," the sisters said.

"Yes, you may try on the sandal," the mayor's representative said. "For the proclamation issued by the mayor said that any girl in Baltimore and surrounding areas may try." He spoke kindly to Cindy Ellie. "Sit down, miss, and see if it fits you." And do you know, that sandal just slid on Cindy Ellie's little foot as smooth as silk. Then she pulled the other sandal from the pocket in her clean but ragged dress.

As soon as she put it on her foot, right there before their very eyes, Cindy Ellie was transformed into the African princess they had seen the two nights before. Them sisters had a fit.

"Oh, Cindy Ellie, we didn't mean you no harm! Oh, Cindy Ellie, please forgive us!" They was on the floor, rolling around and carrying on.

Cindy Ellie told them, "Get up off that floor, and stop all that whooping and hollering. I forgive you."

Then Cindy Ellie was transported to the mayor's mansion in his private limousine. Toussaint was there, waiting to welcome her with open arms. Cindy Ellie was true to her word. For she forgave her stepsisters not only in word but also in deed: she found them two ugly councilmen for husbands. Toussaint and Cindy Ellie were married in the biggest Baptist church in East Baltimore, and the reception was held in the Convention Center. And they lived happily, happily, forever after.

Mary Carter Smith, a 17-year storytelling veteran, is the official griot of the state of Maryland. She is a co-founder of the Association of Black Storytellers and has visited Africa seven times. Smith lives in Baltimore.

CAP O' RUSHES

Ellin Greene

Well, there was once a very rich gentleman, and he had three daughters, and he thought he'd see how fond they were of him. So he said to the first, "How much do you love me, my dear?"

"Why," said she, "as I love my life."

"That's good," said he.

So he said to the second, "How much do *you* love me, my dear?"

"Why," said she, "better than all the world."

"That's good," said he.

So he said to the third, "How much do y*ou* love me, my dear?"

"Why, I love you as fresh meat loves salt," said she.

Well, but he was angry. "You don't love me at all," said he, "and in my house you'll stay no more." So he drove her out there and then and shut the door in her face.

Well, she went away, on and on till she came to a fen, and there she gathered a lot of rushes and made them into a sort of cloak with a hood to cover her from head to foot and hide her fine clothes. And then she went on and on till she came to a great house.

"Do you want a maid?" said she.

"No, we don't," said they.

"I have nowhere to go," said she, "and I ask no wages and do any sort of work."

"Well," said they, "if you like to wash the pots and scrape the sauce-pans, you may stay."

So she stayed there and washed the pots and scraped the saucepans and did all the dirty work. And because she gave no name, they called her Cap o' Rushes.

Well, one day there was to be a great dance a little way off, and the servants were allowed to go and look on at the grand people. Cap o' Rushes said she was too tired to go, so she stayed at home.

But when they were gone, she offed with her cap o' rushes and

I have loved this story since the day I discovered it in Joseph Jacobs's English Folk and Fairy Tales *early in my storytelling career. It reminds me of the strong love but also the frequent misunderstandings between my father and me during my childhood and adolescence and the sweet joy of reconciliation that we shared as adults.*

cleaned herself and went to the dance. And no one there was so finely dressed as she.

Well, who should be there but her master's son, and what should he do but fall in love with her the minute he set eyes on her. He wouldn't dance with anyone else.

But before the dance was done, Cap o' Rushes slipped off, and away she went home. When the other maids came back, she was pretending to be asleep with her cap o' rushes on.

Well, next morning they said to her, "You did miss a sight, Cap o' Rushes!"

"What was that?" said she.

"Why, the most beautiful lady you ever did see, dressed right gay and ga'. The young master, he never took his eyes off her."

"Well, I should have liked to have seen her," said Cap o' Rushes.

"Well, there's to be another dance this evening, and perhaps she'll be there."

But come the evening, Cap o' Rushes said she was too tired to go with them. Howsoever, when they were gone, she offed with her cap o' rushes and cleaned herself, and away she went to the dance.

The master's son had been reckoning on seeing her, and he danced with no one else and never took his eyes off her. But before the dance was over, she slipped off, and home she went, and when the maids came back, she pretended to be asleep with her cap o' rushes on.

Next day they said to her again, "Well, Cap o' Rushes, you should have been there to see the lady. There she was again, gay and ga', and the young master, he never took his eyes off her."

"Well," said she, "I should have liked to have seen her."

"Well," said they, "there's a dance again this evening, and you must go with us, for she's sure to be there."

Well, come the evening, Cap o' Rushes said she was too tired to go, and do what they would, she stayed at home. But when they were gone, she offed her cap o' rushes and cleaned herself, and away she went to the dance.

The master's son was rarely glad when he saw her. He danced with none but her and never took his eyes off her. When she wouldn't tell him her name nor where she came from, he gave her a ring and told her if he didn't see her again, he should die.

Well, before the dance was over, off she slipped, and home she went, and when the maids came home, she was pretending to be asleep with her cap o' rushes on.

Well, next day they said to her, "There, Cap o' Rushes, you didn't come last night, and now you won't see the lady, for there's no more dances."

"Well, I should have rarely liked to have seen her," said she.

The master's son tried every way to find out where the lady was gone, but go where he might and ask whom he might, he never heard anything about her. And he got worse and worse for the love of her till he had to keep his bed.

"Make some gruel for the young master," they said to the cook. "He's dying for the love of the lady." The cook had set about making it when Cap o' Rushes came in.

"What are you a-doing of?" said she.

"I'm going to make some gruel for the young master," said the cook. "He's dying for love of the lady."

"Let me make it," said Cap o' Rushes

Well, the cook wouldn't at first, but at last she said yes, and Cap o' Rushes made the gruel. And when she had made it, she slipped the ring into it on the sly before the cook took it upstairs.

The young man drank it, and then he saw the ring at the bottom.

"Send for the cook," said he.

So up she came.

"Who made this gruel here?" said he.

"I did," said the cook, for she was frightened.

The master's son looked at her. "No, you didn't," said he. "Say who did it, and you shan't be harmed."

"Well, then, 'twas Cap o' Rushes," said she.

"Send Cap o' Rushes here," said he.

So Cap o' Rushes came.

"Did you make my gruel?" said he.

"Yes, I did," said she.

"Where did you get this ring?" said he.

"From him who gave it me," said she.

"Who are you, then?" said the young man.

"I'll show you," said she. And she offed with her cap o' rushes, and there she was in her beautiful clothes.

Well, the master's son got well very soon, and they were to be married in a little time. It was to be a very grand wedding, and everyone was asked from far and near. Cap o' Rushes' father was asked. But she had never told anybody who she was.

Before the wedding she went to the cook and said, "I want you to dress every dish without a mite o' salt."

"That'll be rare nasty," said the cook.

"That doesn't signify," said she.

"Very well," said the cook.

Well, the wedding day came, and they were married. And after they were married, all the company sat down to the dinner. When they began to eat the meat, it was so tasteless they couldn't finish it. Cap o' Rushes' father tried first one dish and then another, and then he burst out crying.

"What is the matter?" said the master's son to him.

"Oh!" said he, "I had a daughter. And I asked her how much she loved me. She said, 'As much as fresh meat loves salt.' I turned her from my door, for I thought she didn't love me. But now I see she loved me best of all. And she may be dead, for aught I know."

"No, Father, here she is!" said Cap o' Rushes. And she went up to him and put her arms 'round him.

And so they were all happy ever after.

Ellin Greene of Point Pleasant, New Jersey, is a co-author, with Augusta Baker, of Storytelling: Art and Technique. *She has worked as a storytelling specialist for the New York Public Library and an associate professor at the University of Chicago Graduate Library School.*

THE LEGEND
OF CHARLEY PARKHURST

Hector Lee

I first created this story many years ago for a television storytelling series, and I still enjoy telling it. I've found that it pleases listeners, as well as readers, because it is a folk legend taken straight from history, with intriguing characters, a suspenseful plot, and a surprise ending.

Charley Parkhurst was dying. The old fellow lay unattended on his crude wooden bed in the little cabin where he had spent his latter days as a recluse. The people of Watsonville were vaguely aware of him as a queer sort of duck who preferred to live alone, and few knew or cared that before making this final stop Charley Parkhurst had been one of the two or three most famous stagecoach drivers in the West.

His one known friend, George Harmon, came down from Soquel once in a while just to see how he was getting along, but Charley always refused Harmon's repeated offers of help. When the aging hermit grew too sick to get about, and Harmon realized that he couldn't last much longer, he said again what he had often said before: "Charley, I think you'd better let me call in the doctor; he might be able to help you."

"Hell, no," snorted Charley. "Ain't no doctor goin' to come poking around at me. I know I'm a goner, so let it be. Dyin' is a one-way ticket for a ride you have to take alone. Any damn doctor comes nosin' around here, I'll blow his head off." And that was that. Charley died alone, and his shrunken old body was discovered when Harmon came along a day or two later. The date of death was officially noted as December 28, 1879.

Not much was ever found out about Charley's early years. It was said that he had been born in New Hampshire in 1812 and as a child had worked with his uncle on a farm. But the work was dull, the uncle was strict, and the lad had a mind of his own. He ran away from home. In Providence, Rhode Island, he got a job as a stable boy and coachman for a Mr. Childs and later for a man named Ebenezer Bach, who taught him to manage horses and also how to care for and love them. Eventually, he went to Georgia, where he became a stage driver, and when his employer, Jim Birch, came west to operate a stage line known as the California Stage Company, Charley came along. "I aim to be the best damn driver in California," he said, and he meant it.

The first run was between Oakland and San Jose. The driving was simple. The ground was level, the roads were good, and four horses could easily pull the coach at a fast clip. But during the Gold Rush of the 1850s and '60s the Mother Lode country was calling, and Charley responded. In middle age now, Charley had both the necessary experience and the daring that comes only with the utmost self-confidence. From Stockton to Mariposa and Sacramento to Placerville the roads were rough, the hills steep, and the passages narrow, with sharp curves. The danger of rolling boulders or washouts always lurked unexpectedly ahead.

On such roads it took a team of six horses to bring the swaying, bucking, sometimes top-heavy coach up through the mountains. Coming downhill over such roads called for great strength at the brakes, judgment in matching speed to terrain, and skill in keeping the leaders their distance ahead of the swing team. Good drivers were scarce, the pay was good, and a kind of aristocracy emerged among them. Charley gained the recognition he wanted as one of the best.

In physical appearance he was strong and stocky, about five-and-a-half feet tall. His barrel-chested upper torso, broad bottom, small hands, and short legs gave him an antlike configuration, and like that worthy creature, his sting was sharp. Once a smart-aleck driver, trying to be clever, said, "Charley, it's four o'clock and time for you to get that heavy beam of yours up into the dickey seat."

Charley snapped back, "You'd be broad in the beam too, if you'd drove as many miles as I have. Ain't no snaky slither-hips like you ever goin' to outlast me on a tough run, so you can just put that in your pipe and smoke it, and keep your compliments to yourself." The joker accepted the rebuke, and that ended the raillery.

Although Charley could get as dirty as the next one around the corral or when the roads were axle-deep with mud, he took pride in neatness and style when he appeared in the saloon, the boarding house, or the station before departure. His gloves were made of the finest buckskin that the Indians could fashion to his order, with wide gauntlets decorated with beads, embroidery, or colored silk ornaments. His hats were of felt, with a low crown, a medium brim, and a fancy band of snake skin or leather studded with silver. He wore a handkerchief about the neck, as did all the drivers, for protection against the dust in summer and the friction of the coat collar in winter. His feet were small, but his custom-made boots had three-inch heels that compensated for his lack of height. His face was dark brown, leathery, and tough, but whether this swarthiness was due to some racial mixture or merely prolonged exposure to weather, no one knew or cared to guess.

Up and down the Sierra and throughout the Big Valley all the drivers knew one another. Their bonds of fellowship, forged by the work, were constantly reinforced by their mutual social life at the stations that marked division points along their routes or in major towns where normal runs would begin and end, such as Sacramento, Hang Town-turned-Placerville, Jackson, Sonora, Mariposa, and Merced. At favorite saloons in such places this fraternity, sometimes called the Knights of the Whip, would assemble at night to drink beer or harder stuff, smoke cigars, and talk over their adventures on the road.

Charley rarely smiled. Although he would join the group and drink his share of beer with them, he always remained aloof, and his occasional acid remarks were usually aimed at stopping a topic of conversation rather than adding to it. One time in Jackson the boys were talking about a cargo of special passengers one of them had brought in. They were a small troupe of women accompanied by their "manager," who escorted them from camp to camp for the purpose of putting on shows for the miners. The ladies would dress in provocative costumes, sing, and dance for the enjoyment of the saloon customers, and afterward they were free to pursue such other profitable enterprises as temptation might put in their way.

"That's one covey of quail you shore ought to see. They're really highfalutin," one driver commented. Charley grunted but said nothing. Another driver, Watson by name, thought he would have a little fun on this salacious subject. "Hey, Charley," he taunted, "you ought to hook up with one of them pretty hurdy-gurdy girls and settle down. I hear they make good wives once you get 'em broke-in to a one-team harness." But Charley did not rise to the bait. The ensuing silence rankled Watson, and he could not let the matter drop. He turned to the other grinning members of the clan. "Well, fellers, I guess old Charley ain't been wised up yet; his education seems to be limited to horses. Leastwise, he don't know much about women."

"You might be surprised," cracked Charley. "You don't know half as much as you think you do, yourself. If guts was brains, you'd be a genius. But if it'll make you any wiser, I'll buy the next round of beer." And that ended that conversation.

The drivers never took the hazards of their job lightly, nor did they forget the passengers' comfort and safety or the necessity of faithfully delivering the mail and express shipments. A station agent who dispatched a stage had to be alert for dangerous weather conditions, the possibility of washouts, and the likelihood that sooner or later some highwayman would be lurking at a bend in the road with the intent of lightening the coach and the passengers' burden. Before each departure the agent and driver would hold an informal conference on such matters.

On one occasion the agent warned Charley not to make the run because of the weather, but he chose to go anyway. That winter the snowpack in the mountains had been unusually heavy, and when spring came, the runoff from the melting snow filled the rivers. Recent heavy rains had made matters worse, and floods were inevitable. The Tuolumne River had swollen over its banks in the valleys and was savagely cutting away its walls in the canyons, roaring down like the boring force from a nozzle, bringing trees and other debris with it.

The bridge below Big Oak Flat was in danger of being washed out, and Charley knew that it was only a matter of time. He gave the horses their head, and the coach careened down the narrow road toward the river. As they rounded a curve, Charley and his one passenger could see the raging flood just below them. The bridge was about 50 yards away. Suddenly, in the middle of the road ahead a stranger appeared, waving his arms and shouting against the roar of the torrent. Charley pulled the horses to a sliding stop.

"You better not try to cross that bridge," screamed the obviously frightened man. "She's about to go any minute!"

Charley looked at his passenger and then at the valuable express box he had to deliver.

"Don't go!" pleaded the passenger. "I can wait. We can't take the chance. Let's go back!"

The driver hesitated, struggling silently between common sense and honor. After a tense instant of silence, he had made his decision. Charley let out a screeching Rebel yell, cracked the whip, and with a twist of the wrists took a double hitch on the reins. The little coach shot forward, down to the swaying bridge. With nostrils wide and ears back, the six horses hit the boards of the bridge almost as one. The wheels skidded as they made the curve and slammed onto the shuddering planks. Logs and brush had lodged against the bridge, and water was beginning to rush over it.

The coach hurtled across, then came to a stop on the other side. At that moment, with a squeaking cry, the bridge tore from its moorings and was swept away in the foaming torrent. Charley and the passenger watched it go.

"Good Lord!" the passenger gasped in relief. "I thought we were goners for sure. Another second and we would have been down there in that water, me and you both."

"Aw, hell," snorted Charley. "I'd never let that happen. I'm particular who I take a bath with." The passenger and the strongbox were delivered on time.

Calamities of nature were not the only hazards of the road. The drivers also had to contend with highwaymen. One such character was an enterprising entrepreneur of the road who came to be called Sugarfoot. Not much is known about him, but in the folklore of the region it is said that on two occasions he and Charley Parkhurst came face-to-face.

The first time, Charley was on the Mariposa-to-Stockton run and carrying a large sum of gold in the strongbox under the driver's seat. It was a hot summer day, and Charley's mind was probably on that cool glass of beer that awaited him in the next town. Suddenly, two bandits with covered faces stepped out from behind a large rock. One grabbed the lead horses, and the other leveled a double-barreled shotgun at Charley.

"Now, don't try to be a hero, Charley," the holdup man cautioned. "All we want is the box, so toss 'er down, and no foolishness about it."

"Foolishness, hell!" Charley snorted. "I was asleep, or you wouldn't have got this far. I take it you'd be Sugarfoot, you low-down . . . " The unprintable epithets were cut short by the bandit.

"You might be right. You just tell 'em old Sugarfoot got the last laugh on you this time."

"Well, this'll be the last time," mumbled Charley as he threw down the box. "Next time you try this on me, I'll put daylight through that yellow liver of yours, and that's no lie."

So the outlaws got the gold, and Charley smarted from the embarrassment of it. The next day he slipped a loaded pistol under the driver's seat and thereafter never made a run without it.

A few months later the showdown came. On the same run and almost at the same place, the two masked gunmen suddenly appeared again and waved the horses to a stop. The express box was carrying more gold than usual, and this time Charley was not taken by surprise. The outlaws gave the order for him to toss down the box. Pretending to comply, Charley reached down for the heavy chest, but in the same movement he suddenly jerked on the reins. The lead team reared back, while the other horses jostled in confusion. During the momentary distraction, both bandits looked at the horses. Charley came up with the gun, and two quick shots cracked out. One outlaw dropped his shotgun and grabbed his stomach. The other dodged in the bushes, jumped on his horse, and clattered off up the rocky hillside.

The wounded man stumbled to his horse and managed to get away, but a few days later he was found dying in an abandoned miner's cabin not far away. He was identified as Sugarfoot.

At one stage in his career—some say it happened near Redwood City—Charley met with the kind of accident that all drivers dreaded: he was kicked in the face while trying to shoe a horse. He lost the sight of his left eye, and for the rest of his life he wore a patch over it. From then on, people called him One-Eyed Charley, but not in his presence, of course.

In 1867 Charley established his final residence in Santa Cruz County. Accordingly, he registered his citizenship there as Charley Darkey Parkhurst; age 55; occupation, farmer; native of New Hampshire; residence, Soquel. There is no evidence to show whether "Darkey" was a family name or a pejorative epithet, but apparently it was legal enough; he voted in the 1868 national election.

Aging or used-up stage drivers had no future to look forward to, but the time for Charley's retirement finally came. Rheumatism had made driving difficult for him, wages were going down, and he had begun to think of a better life. With his savings he was able to buy a small ranch near Soquel, and there he raised apples, wheat, hay, and a few cattle. But the increasing pain of rheumatism and a rapidly developing cancer of the tongue rendered him helpless, and he had to sell the ranch. He moved to a small cabin near Watsonville, where kind folks could look in on him occasionally.

He had lived a most colorful life. Known far and wide as one of the best whips of the Gold Rush days, he had enjoyed the professional respect of his peers. He had killed an outlaw and thus gained a moment of fame. He had rolled dice for drinks, chewed tobacco, smoked cigars, and gambled in the saloons with the toughest of his kind. Yet he was fiercely independent and refused medical aid even in the last painful days of his life. Despite his renown, he was always a loner and seemed to relish the shadows of mystery that enveloped him.

He died alone, and his secrets followed him almost to the grave. But when George Harmon discovered Charley's small, twisted body and the coroner was called, his greatest secret was revealed. Charley Parkhurst was a woman.

Hector Lee of Santa Rosa, California, is a professor emeritus of English at Sonoma State University and a former president of the California Folklore Society. He is the author of several books on American and Western folklore, and in the 1950s and '60s he presented television and radio storytelling programs.

ONE DAY, ONE NIGHT

Joe Hayes

Here is a story that takes us clear back to the beginning of time. Back then there wasn't the steady rhythm of days and nights such as we have now. Instead, it might be dark for 10 years in a row, and then light for just one day. It might be dark for eight long years. Then light for one day.

Now, some of the animals liked it fine that way. But there were other animals who were very unhappy. The rabbit, for example, was one very unhappy animal. She would feel a lot safer if she could see her enemies creeping up on her.

The squirrel was unhappy too. She liked to run down one branch to the very end and then take a long flying jump to another branch and run up that one. But in the darkness the squirrel would miss the second branch and fall and hit her head almost every time.

The birds didn't like it either. Well, one bird—the owl—was happy, but not the rest of them. Even the hawk and the eagle were unhappy because they could hunt better when it was light out.

So one day when the sun happened to be out, Eagle flew clear up to the sun and told him that many animals were unhappy. There wasn't enough daylight. The sun said that he wanted all the animals to be happy. He said that Eagle should call the animals together and let them talk about it. However they wanted things to be—however much daylight and darkness—the sun said he would make things that way.

So Eagle flew down and called the animals to a meeting. Each animal stood up and said how he thought things should be arranged.

The biggest and strongest animals were the first to speak. Bear stood up and growled, "Ten years of darkness . . . one day!"

Some of the animals agreed with Bear. But the other animals had different ideas. Skunk said, "I think that there should be four years of darkness and . . . two days."

Badger mumbled, "Aw, why can't it just be dark all the time?"

But Rabbit stood up and said, "No! It should be light all the time."

And Bluebird chirped, "My children need daylight."

There were many different ideas. And the last one to speak was Frog. Frog had an idea no one else had thought of. He stood up and croaked, "One day . . . one night. One day . . . one night."

Right away most of the animals saw that was the best idea of all. The day and the night should just follow one another like black and white beads along a string.

But Bear wasn't going to let that weak little frog tell him how things should be. He kept growling, "Ten years of darkness . . . one day!"

Before long all the animals were divided into two groups—the few who agreed with Bear, and all the rest, who agreed with Frog.

Eagle had to fly clear back to the sun and tell him that now the animals were in two groups and couldn't settle their difference. Sun said there was only one thing to do. They should have a contest. Each group should pick an animal to speak for it. The animal who could say what he wanted the longest without stopping would have things his way.

Eagle told the animals what the sun had said. Right away Bear said he would talk for his group. And you should have heard him laugh when he heard that Frog would speak for the other group. Bear thought he could roar so loud that no one would ever hear Frog.

When the time for the contest arrived, Bear went and stood on one bank of a river. Frog hopped out onto the other bank. Bear didn't even wait for the signal to begin. Right away he began to growl, "Ten years of darkness . . . one day!"

When the signal came, Frog croaked, "One day . . . one night. One day . . . one night."

At first it looked like Bear was right. Frog could hardly be heard. But you know, Bear was not really used to talking all the time. His throat began to get sore, and his voice grew hoarse. Bear dipped a paw into the river and scooped up a drink of water. His voice came back strong: "Ten years of darkness . . . one day!" But his voice didn't come back for long. He started losing it again. And the next thing you know, Bear's mouth was moving, but there wasn't a sound coming out.

But on the other bank of the river, Frog was just getting warmed up! "One day . . . one night. One day . . . one night."

Finally, Bear had to admit he had been beaten. He stalked off, muttering to himself. But Frog never did stop talking. To this day you can go outside on a warm evening and hear Frog talking out there by the water. If you could speak his language, you would hear him say, "One day . . . one night. One day . . . one night."

But as you probably know, when the weather turns cool, Frog hides under a rock and goes to sleep. When the frog has gone to sleep, Bear starts growling again: "Ten years of darkness . . . one day!"

The sun hears the bear growling, and Sun is a little frightened of Bear. The sun starts traveling a little more quickly across the sky each day. That makes the days get shorter and shorter.

But when the really cold weather sets in, Bear hunts up a cave in the mountains, and he goes to sleep. After Bear has gone to sleep, the sun grows braver and starts traveling a little more slowly across the sky each day. The days get longer and longer.

Now, that all happened a long time ago, but there is one more thing you should know about it. Ever since then, among the animals, and especially among the people, it isn't the one who is biggest and loudest and strongest who gets things his way. The one who gets things his way is the one who says what he wants over and over and over.

Joe Hayes of Santa Fe, New Mexico, grew up in Arizona and was fascinated with the tales of the American Southwest. He began his storytelling career by sharing those stories with his own children, and in 1980 he became a professional teller.

FLOWERS AND FRECKLE CREAM

Elizabeth Ellis

When I was a kid about 12 years old, I was already as tall as I am now, and I had a lot of freckles. I had reached the age when I had begun to really look at myself in the mirror, and I was underwhelmed. Apparently my mother was too, because sometimes she'd look at me and shake her head and say, "You can't make a silk purse out of a sow's ear."

I had a cousin whose name was Janette Elizabeth, and Janette Elizabeth looked exactly like her name sounds. She had a waist so small that men could put their hands around it . . . and they did. She had waist-length naturally curly blonde hair too, but to me her unforgivable sin was that she had a flawless peaches-and-cream complexion. I couldn't help comparing myself with her and thinking that my life would be a lot different if I had beautiful skin too—skin that was all one color.

And then, in the back pages of Janette Elizabeth's *True Confessions* magazine, I found the answer: an advertisement for freckle-remover cream. I knew that I could afford it if I saved my money, and I did. The ad assured me that the product would arrive in a "plain brown wrapper." Plain brown freckle color.

For three weeks I went to the mailbox every day precisely at the time the mail was delivered. I knew that if someone else in my family got the mail, I would never hear the end of it. There was no way that they would let me open the box in private. Finally, after three weeks of scheduling my entire day around the mail truck's arrival, my package came.

I went to my room with it, sat on the edge of my bed, and opened it. I was sure that I was looking at a miracle. But I had gotten so worked up about the magical package that I couldn't bring myself to put the cream on. What if it didn't work? What would I do then?

I fell asleep that night without even trying the stuff. And when I got up the next morning and looked at my freckles in the mirror, I said, "Elizabeth, this is silly. You have to do it now!" I smeared the cream all over my body. There wasn't as much of it as I had thought there would be,

My maternal grandfather, Issac Hugh Gabbard, was a circuit-riding minister from the turn of the century until well into the 1950s. He gave me wonderful gifts: the love of stories and the ability to see the beauty in everyone, including myself. Each year I spent my summer in Kentucky with him. This is the story of one of those summers.

and I could see that I was going to need a part-time job to keep me in freckle remover.

Later that day I took my hoe and went with my brother and cousins to the head of the holler to hoe tobacco, as we did nearly every day in the summer. Of course, when you stay out hoeing tobacco all day, you're not working in the shade. And there was something important I hadn't realized about freckle remover: if you wear it in the sun, it seems to have a reverse effect. Instead of developing a peaches-and-cream complexion, you just get more and darker freckles.

By the end of the day I looked as though I had leopard blood in my veins, although I didn't realize it yet. When I came back to the house, my family, knowing nothing about the freckle-remover cream, began to say things like, "I've never seen you with that many freckles before." When I saw myself in the mirror, I dissolved into tears and hid in the bathroom.

My mother called me to the dinner table, but I ignored her. When she came to the bathroom door and demanded that I come out and eat, I burst out the door and ran by her, crying. I ran out to the well house and threw myself down, and I was still sobbing when my grandfather came out to see what was wrong with me. I told him about how I'd sent for the freckle remover, and he didn't laugh—though he did suggest that one might get equally good results from burying a dead black cat when the moon was full.

It was clear that Grandpa didn't understand, so I tried to explain why I didn't want to have freckles and why I felt so inadequate when I compared my appearance with Janette Elizabeth's. He looked at me in stunned surprise, shook his head, and said, "But child, there are all kinds of flowers, and they are all beautiful." I said, "I've never seen a flower with freckles!" and ran back to my room, slamming the door.

When my mother came and knocked, I told her to go away. She started to say the kinds of things that parents say at times like that, but my grandfather said, "Nancy, leave the child alone." She was a grown-up, but he was her father. So she left me alone.

I don't know where Grandpa found it. It isn't at all common in the mountains where we lived then. But I know he put it in my room because my mother told me later. I had cried myself to sleep that night, and when I opened my swollen, sticky eyes the next morning, the first thing I saw, lying on the pillow next to my head, was a tiger lily.

Elizabeth Ellis grew up in the Appalachian Mountains and began her storytelling career while working as a librarian in Dallas, where she now lives. She became a full-time professional teller in 1978 and enjoys sharing tales about heroic American women.

THE PRINCESS AND THE DOVE

Mary Hamilton

One morning a princess sat by the open window of her second-story bedroom, combing her long beautiful hair. Suddenly, a dove flew down, picked up in its beak a barrette she had intended to place in her hair, and flew away.

The next morning the princess sat by the same window, combing her long beautiful hair. And suddenly, the same dove flew down, picked up in its beak a scarf she had intended to place in her hair, and flew away.

The following morning the princess sat by the same window. She had just finished combing her long beautiful hair when, suddenly, the same dove flew down, picked up her comb in its beak, and flew away.

The princess said, "That does it!" She stood up, marched out of the palace, and went off in search of the dove.

The dove would fly ahead, stop, and wait for her to catch up, fly ahead and wait, fly ahead and wait, fly ahead and wait, fly, wait, fly, wait. In that way the dove led the princess deep into the forest—to places she had never been before. Then the dove disappeared.

The princess kept walking and soon came to a clearing. On the far side of the clearing stood a really miserable-looking hut. But from out of the hut walked the most handsome young man the princess had ever seen.

She said, "Hi! I'm a princess from a palace back that way somewhere. And I was just wondering, did you, by any chance, see a dove fly by here? It would have been carrying a comb in its beak. You see, it's been stealing from me for the past three days, and today it stole my comb. Did you see a dove like that?"

The young man said, "I know all about that dove. You see, I am that dove. I'm under a spell. I don't know how or why I came to be under the spell, but I have learned that you, and only you, can break it. That is why I led you out here."

"Me? Only me? What do I have to do?"

"All you have to do is sit in the chair that's just inside that open window. The next time I turn into a dove, I'll fly off over that mountain, and you must watch the spot where I disappear for one full year, one month, and one day, and then I'll never have to be a dove again."

"Are you sure I'm the only one?"

"Yes. I don't know how or why I came to be under the spell, but I do know you are the only one who can break it."

Without another word, the princess took her place in the chair. The next time the man turned into a dove, he flew off over the mountain. And she began to watch the spot where he had disappeared.

The sun shone in on her, and her skin burned and cracked and peeled, cracked and peeled, cracked and peeled, cracked and peeled, until it looked more like tree bark than skin. Animals came and lived in her clothing. Animals came and lived in her hair. She was rained upon; she was snowed upon; she was sleeted upon. But for one full year, one month, and one day, she did not take her eyes from that spot.

Then he came walking back. When he saw how hideous she had become, he said, "Look at you. You did all this for a man?" Then "Pppt," he spit on her and walked away.

She could not believe it. She had been sitting in the chair for so long that she couldn't even stand up. She slid off her chair and pulled herself out of the hut and across the clearing, where she collapsed in tears under a tree. She cried and she cried until she had cried herself to sleep. She slept for a very long time.

When she awoke, there were three older women with her who said, "We know—we know what happened to you, and we're going to help you make everything right." The first of the women touched her hair, and her hair became more beautiful than it had ever been. The second woman touched her skin, and her skin became more beautiful than it had ever been. The third woman touched her clothing, and her clothes became the most beautiful ones the princess had ever seen. Then, instantly, she was living in a palace, and the three older women were there as her handmaidens.

Now, it happened that her palace was next door to the palace where the young man who had been a dove was now a king. The next morning the king woke up and saw a palace next door that hadn't been there the night before. But before he could decide what to do about the palace, he saw, walking past the windows of the palace, the most beautiful woman he had ever seen. He knew he had to have her. He sent a servant next door to see if they might meet.

The servant came back, saying, "Your Majesty, she says that, yes, the two of you may meet, but only under the following conditions: You must build a platform from the balcony of her palace to the balcony of your palace. The platform must be covered two inches thick with rose petals. You must stand on your balcony. You may not set foot on the platform. You may not speak. She will walk from her balcony to your balcony, and the two of you will meet."

The king ordered his carpenters to begin building the platform. He told all his other subjects to stop whatever they were doing and to go out and gather rose petals. In time the platform was ready.

When it was, the king stood on his balcony, taking care not to set foot on the platform and not to speak. The princess stood on her balcony with her handmaidens, who said to her, "All right, this is how it works. You start walking across the platform. When you're about one-third of the way across, pretend to step on a thorn, fall down, pretend to faint, and leave everything else to us."

She said, "Sounds fine," and started walking across the platform. When she was about one-third of the way across, she cried, "Oh, it's a thorn in my foot. You're trying to kill me!" She fell down and pretended to faint. The handmaidens came out, picked her up, and dragged her back, glaring at the king the entire time.

The king was beside himself. He wasn't allowed to set foot on the platform; he wasn't allowed to speak. He stood and watched, waited and watched, waited and watched. He saw doctors coming and going and coming and going from her palace. The rumors flew: "She's dying, she's dying." He saw a priest come over; he saw a bishop come over; he was sure she was going to die at any moment.

After a few days went by, this rumor came over: "No, she's not going to die, but her foot, indeed, her whole leg, is swollen to 40 times its normal size, and she'll never be the same again."

After a few weeks went by, another rumor came over: "The swelling's gone down; she's going to be all right."

The king decided to try again. He sent another servant over to see if they might meet. The servant came back, saying, "Your Majesty, she says that yes, the two of you may meet, but only under the following conditions: You must tear down that horrid platform with the thorn in it and build a new platform in its place. The new platform must be covered three inches thick with jasmine petals. Again you must stand on your balcony; you may not set foot on the platform; you may not speak. She will walk from her balcony to your balcony, and the two of you will meet."

The king ordered his carpenters to tear down the old platform and build a new one, and in time all was ready. When it was, the king stood on his balcony, taking care not to set foot on the platform and not to speak.

The princess stood over on her balcony. Her handmaidens were there with her, and they said, "You know how it works. This time, go about halfway across before you find the thorn."

She said, "Sounds fine," and she gave the king a big smile and a little wave and then started walking across the platform. When she was about halfway across, she cried, "Oh! It's another thorn. Now I'm sure you're trying to kill me!" She fell down and pretended to faint. The handmaidens came out, picked her up, and dragged her back, glaring at the king the entire time.

Again the king was beside himself. Again the rumors flew: "She's dying. She's dying. No, her foot, indeed, her whole leg is swollen to 40 times its normal size." After many months went by, this rumor came over: "The swelling's gone down. She's going to be all right."

The king decided to try one more time. He sent another servant over to see if they might meet. That servant came back, saying, "Your Majesty, she says she does not want to set eyes on you until you are stretched out in your coffin."

The king sent for his coffin-makers and had a coffin made to his exact size and shape, leaving off the lid, of course. Then he climbed in and stretched out in his coffin.

He had his servants lift the coffin and carry it through the city, saying, "Come see the king in his coffin. Come see the king in his coffin."

The princess stood on her balcony, and she waited. When the king came by in his coffin, she said, "Look at you. You did all this for a woman?" Then "Pppt," she spit on him.

Somehow those words seemed vaguely familiar to the king. Then he took the first close look he had really taken at her. He saw that, indeed, she was the woman who had been the girl who had so willingly sat for a year, a month, and a day to break a spell for him.

So he climbed out of his coffin, went over to her, and said, "First, will you please forgive me for the way I treated you in the forest? And second, could we start over?"

So she forgave him, and starting over is exactly what they did.

Mary Hamilton, a former high school English teacher, began telling stories full time in 1983. In the past decade Hamilton has developed a repertoire of folk tales from around the world. She lives in Louisville, Kentucky.

THE FIRST MOTORCYCLE IN BLACK MOUNTAIN

David Holt

Now, after the Second World War, most folks in Black Mountain, North Carolina, had *heard* of motorcycles, but they'd never *seen* one. So when old Leroy Teats arrived home from the Navy with his brand-new blue and chrome Harley-Davidson motorcycle, folks come a-runnin' out of their homes and out of their stores to see what was making all that racket.

Why, it was a sight to behold. Had a headlight big as a dinner plate and a seat wide as a buckboard, and—in the very back—it had a big old ruby-studded mud flap. It had a windshield that came almost as high as Leroy's head, and some folks said that thing was even *air-conditioned*. They could tell Leroy was happy and proud . . . all they had to do was count the bugs on his teeth.

Wasn't long, though, before some of those mountain boys came up and started teasin' and tauntin' him.

"What *is* that big old thing, Leroy? Why, you can't take it out on these mountain roads. It's too shiny, just a play-pretty. It looks like a pregnant bicycle."

Leroy said, "I can take this motorcycle anywhere in the county, and I mean *anywhere!*"

About that time, Jeter Ledford walked up, leading his mule. He said, "Leroy, I bet you can't take that thing where my mule can go."

"I can too," said Leroy. "I can take this motorcycle *anywhere* your old mule can go."

"All right," said Jeter, "let me see you take it up to the top of High Windy, 'cause I have rid my mule straight up to the top, and there's no road. It's just trees, rocks, sticks, and leaves all the way."

Leroy started her up. VROOOOOM! He had to have it in full throttle and hold on for all he was worth just to stay on the mountain. The crowd all hollered out, "We'll watch for you, Leroy!"

Now, what they all forgot about was Rhubarb Golightly, who lived way up at the top of High Windy. Rhubarb hadn't been to town in seven years

I first heard this story from Grover Norwood, a native of Black Mountain, North Carolina, and one of those rare natural storytellers. Of course, the tale itself is an old joke, but Grover fleshed it out with local names, places, and personalities, turning it into a full-blown tale. I blew it up a little more, and here it is.

and didn't care if he ever went to town again. He just lived up there with his wife, Samanthy. They did all their own chores and were used to hearing the sounds of birds and bees and things like that. They had never even heard tell of a motorcycle.

So that day, when old Rhubarb Golightly had just finished his big dinner of biscuits and red-eye gravy, skunk cabbage, poke salad, sowbelly gravy with chitlins, bean pie with possum sauce, and sweet taters—topped off with some crab-apple pudding and two jaw-shrinking dill pickles—he sat down on the front porch to take his ease . . . when he heard something coming up through the woods. VROOM! VROOM! Rhubarb had never knowed a man or a bear or a dog to make a sound like that. Then he saw it coming. That headlight was just a-flashin', that engine just a-spittin'. There were rocks and sticks flyin', dogs runnin', and chickens cacklin', PLK! PLK! PLK!

Rhubarb jumped up and hollered, "Samanthy, Samanthy—bring me my gun!"

She ran outside with his big old shotgun. He leveled that thing and fired. BOOM! BOOM! Leroy went flying one way, and the motorcycle flew the other.

Samanthy said, "Did you kill it, honey?"

"I don't know," says Rhubarb, "but whatever it was, I sure made it turn that boy loose!"

David Holt was born in Texas, but as a young man he felt drawn to the music and lore of the Southern Appalachian Mountains. In 1975 he founded the Appalachian Music Program at Warren Wilson College in Asheville, North Carolina, and he has won awards for both his storytelling and his musical performances. Holt is frequently featured on television's Nashville Network and lives in Fairview, North Carolina.

MARIE JOLIE

J. J. Reneaux

Down in the bayou country there was once a beautiful girl named Marie. She was so pretty, so *jolie*, that all the people called her Marie Jolie. She was as sweet as sugar cane, but if you did her wrong, look out, for that girl could show a temper as hot as cayenne pepper.

Now, Marie Jolie grew to be of a marrying age, but to her maman's disappointment, she wasn't yet of a mind to be married. First she wanted to have adventures and see the big world. So she found something wrong with every young man who came to court her. This one was too short; that one was too tall; the next one had the ears of an *éléphant*.

After a while her maman got impatient with Marie, for she worried that her daughter would wind up an old maid—a terrible fate in those days. So Maman said, "Marie Jolie, it is time for you to take a husband. You can't pick one to suit you, so me, I'm gonna do it for you. We gonna have us a contest. You see this pumpkin? I'm gonna get M'su Carencro, the buzzard, to put it on the highest, skinniest branch of that big cypress tree out there in the swamp. *Chère*, the man who can fetch that pumpkin down without fallin' in the water is gonna be your husband!"

"Well, Maman," said Marie, "if it's got to be, I s'pose that's as good a way as any of choosin' a man."

The contest was held the following week. Men came from parishes far and near, each one more eager than the last to win the hand of Marie Jolie. But one, a tall, dark, handsome man, stood out from the crowd. "Ooh, Maman," said Marie, "I hope he gets the pumpkin! He's a good-lookin' devil for true."

One after the other, the men tried to climb the great cypress, but they all ended up spitting swamp water. At last the good lookin' stranger's turn came. Quick as lightnin' he scaled that tree like a cat, snatched the pumpkin, and landed with his boots on dry land. Before she knew it, Marie Jolie was a married woman.

She climbed proud as could be into her husband's wagon, and they

My grandmaman first told me this story, giving me a hot-tempered heroine to dream of in a time when most little girls were playing Barbie or Suzy Homemaker. Now I tell the story to my daughter, and watching her eyes light up, I know the tale will be lovingly carried and told to yet another generation.

117

started driving down the road. It wasn't long, however, before she noticed that things were getting strange. The path was growing darker and darker, and her new husband uglier and uglier.

Suddenly a fearsome man appeared beside the path. "Gimme my tie and collar that I lent ya!" he called out. Marie's husband took off the tie and collar. "Here, then," he said, "take back your ol' tie and collar!"

A little further down the road, they met another man. He said, "Gimme back my coat that I lent ya!" "Take your ol' coat," said her husband. Yet a third man appeared and demanded his trousers; a fourth demanded his hat. Her husband stopped the wagon, disappeared briefly into the swamp woods, and returned just as well dressed as before.

Finally, a fifth man, fiercer than all the others together, his face hidden in the shadow of his tall hat, appeared before them and pointed a long, bony finger. "Give me the horses that I lent ya!" he roared. "Go to the devil, then," said her husband with a wicked laugh, "and take your ol' horses with ya!"

He watched as the man led the animals away, and then he turned to his wife and hissed, "Girl, get down and hitch y'self to the wagon, and pull us home!" Marie Jolie could feel her temper rising. She was gonna tell him a thing or two! But a terrible change had come over her husband. His icy glare and ugly scowl frightened her. She thought she had better do as he said—at least for a little while. She climbed down, hitched herself to the wagon, and began to pull with all her strength.

At last they arrived at her husband's *cabane*. It was a gloomy lookin' place, set way back in the swamp woods. "Marie Jolie," said her husband, "I must leave. While I am gone, you will stay here, and my maman will take good care of you." And he disappeared in a burst of flames and smoke.

Marie was scared for true. She begged her new mama-in-law, "Please, Belle-mère, tell me why my husband is so strange!"

Belle-mère, who was a kind woman at heart and felt worse than anybody about how her son had turned out, sadly shook her head. "Oh, *chère fille!*" she said, "You've made a terrible match. You have gone and married M'su Diable, the devil himself!"

Marie couldn't believe her ears. "Old woman, you are only jealous. You just want to break up my marriage!"

"You do not believe me, *'tite fille*? Come with me," the old woman whispered. She led Marie Jolie inside the house to a secret door. She unlocked it with a big brass key, and the heavy door creaked open. There inside that dim room Marie saw the devil's other wives—each one hanging from a hook.

Now Marie Jolie knew the truth. "Oh, please, Belle-mère," she cried, "you gotta tell me how I can escape! How can I get out of here?"

"Girl, do you not see what became of the others who tried to escape? Stay with me, little one, I will keep you comp'ny and ease your suffering," Belle-mère pleaded. "Do not bring down the terrible wrath of my son, the devil!"

But Marie Jolie was growing angry, and in her anger she grew bold. "No," she insisted, "I will not be the devil's wife! If you won't help me escape, I'll find a way on my own!"

Belle-mère sighed. "The devil knows many tricks. He can change into fire and smoke and ride the wind. You cannot outrun him, but maybe—if you are brave enough—you can outsmart him. Even the devil cannot defeat a strong heart. But if your courage fails, he will destroy you!"

Marie was determined. "My heart is strong, and my mind is made up," she said. "M'su Diable will not destroy me!"

"All right then," said Belle-mère, "here is what you must do. M'su Diable will return in the deepest night, at three o'clock, the soul's hour. He hates dawn and the rising sun. In its light he cannot hide his true self, so he sleeps. His spy, L'Gaim, the rooster, keeps watch. If he catches you tryin' to escape, he will crow. Tonight you must feed L'Gaim three bags of corn instead of one so that he will oversleep. At sunrise go and gather six dirty eggs. They will protect you. Do not take the clean eggs, for they are bad luck. Then, *chère*, run as quick-quick as you can away from this place!"

Marie did as she was told. Rooster overslept, and she got the six dirty eggs. She tiptoed out, soft-soft, but the gate hinge squeaked, and L'Gaim woke up crowin' full-throat. "M'su Diable, M'su Diable, wake up! *Vite-vite!* Your wife is gettin' away!"

Marie ran for her life as M'su Diable came screaming after her. She had not gone far when she turned and saw a cloud of smoke and fire approaching. She took one dirty egg and threw it over her shoulder. BOOM! It exploded right in the devil's path, and a fence of wood as high and wide as the eye could see sprang up. M'su Diable snorted and stomped in fury and flew back to his *cabane*. When he returned, he had his magic golden ax. The ax chopped through the fence at once, and the devil was again hot on the trial of his runaway wife.

Marie grabbed a second dirty egg and heaved it straight at the devil. CRACK! It flashed like a bolt of lightning, and a fence of brick sprang up as high and wide as the eye could see. The devil cursed and spat, but his magic ax smashed the brick to bits.

Marie took aim and flung the third dirty egg. It shattered like thunder, and a fence of stone sprang up as high and wide as the eye could see. The devil shrieked and set his ax to ripping through the wall, and soon the cloud of fire and smoke again threatened to destroy her.

Marie took the fourth egg and hurled it through the air. The earth shook with its force, and a fence of iron sprang up as high and wide as the eye could see. But it too was little trouble for M'su Diable's fearsome magic.

Marie ran as fast as she could, but M'su Diable was almost upon her. She grabbed the fifth egg and pitched it straight into the fireball behind her. A wall of flames roared to the sky, and a deep bayou appeared before the devil. The water stopped him cold. But suddenly, a great gust of wind blew the evil cloud of smoke and fire over the bayou, and the waters began to boil.

Marie's blood ran cold as ice when she looked back this time. For M'su Diable had dropped his disguise, and now she saw the ol' devil himself as he truly is. His forked tail whipped wildly about, his cloven hooves raised clouds of dust, and his goat beard flapped wickedly in the wind. The bright sun glinted off his sharp, curved horns, and his beady eyes burned like hot coals. Crusty red scales covered his body. For true, M'su Diable looked a whole lot like a boiled crawfish!

Only one dirty egg remained, and Marie threw it with her last ounce of strength. But her hand trembled, so that she completely missed her mark. The egg fell at her own two feet and exploded. The earth rumbled and cracked. A mighty river came rolling by. It was the Mississippi. Marie was trapped. How could she ever swim such a wide, dangerous river?

But wait—wasn't that old Grandmaman Cocodrie [the alligator] sunning herself over there in the shallows? Marie cried out to the gator, *"Te prie, Grandmaman, traversez moi! Grandmaman, te prie sauvez ma vie! Aidez moi, Cocodrie!* Grandmother, I pray you, carry me across. Grandmother, I pray you, save my life! Help me, Old Cocodrie!"

Grandmaman Cocodrie, always on the lookout for an easy meal, swam up to Marie without a moment's hesitation. "Maybe I will carry you across," she growled. "But tell me, what makes you think I won't eat you up?"

"Grandmaman," said Marie, "I'd rather be your supper than be the devil's wife!"

"Climb on my back, *'tite fille*, I like your courage!" said the old alligator, and she carried Marie quickly and safely to the other side.

Just then, M'su Diable came runnin' up to the bank. In his most charming voice he called out, *"Traversez moi, Grandmaman, traversez moi! Belle, belle Cocodrie!* Carry me across, old Grandmother, carry me across! Beautiful, beautiful Cocodrie!"

"Climb on my back, M'su, I'll give you a ride for sure!" said the ol' gator with a snap of her jaws. M'su Diable stepped onto her scaly back, holding his forked tail out of the muddy water, and Grandmaman Cocodrie swam out into the deep river.

Things were looking awfully bad for Marie, with M'su Diable closing in on her. But if there was anything that Grandmaman Cocodrie hated, it was a mean ol' devil on her back, and suddenly, way out where the water was swiftest and darkest, she dived. M'su Diable didn't have a snowball's chance in August. M'su Diable, of course, can't swim a lick—not much water down where he comes from. The Ol' Muddy took that devil kickin' and sputterin' all the way downstream to New Orleans. Some say he washed up in the French Quarter, right smack dab in the middle of Bourbon Street—but then, that's another story altogether.

As for Marie Jolie, she lived to be *une très vieille femme*, a very old woman. She had many adventures before her black hair turned snow white. People began to call her Marie Esprit, the spirited one. When they asked why she never married again, she'd just smile and say, "You know, *chère*, once you been married to one devil, there's no need to go out and look for another one!"

J. J. Reneaux tells stories drawn from her Louisiana Cajun heritage. A storyteller, musician, and singer, she often performs original material in both English and Cajun French. Reneaux lives in Comer, Georgia.

CARNA AND THE BOOTS OF SEVEN STRIDES

Bill Harley

Carna's mother was a strong woman. She had strong arms and strong legs and strong, sure hands. And she had a big heart. When Carna was 12 years old, her mother came to her and said, "Go see your father. Ask him for the skin of the brown bull. I want you to take it to the cobbler at the far edge of town. Tell him you are my daughter and that you want him to make you boots of seven strides. Not six; six is not enough. Not eight, for eight is too many. Boots of seven strides."

"But what are they for?" asked Carna.

"Why," her mother said, "they're for you to see the world and to do what needs to be done. Now go." And with that, her mother went back to work in her garden. In it were thousands of plants. Not just tomato plants and geraniums and marigolds—though she had those too—but rubber plants from Malaysia and sunflowers from Italy and the lichen that the reindeer on the Norwegian tundra ate.

Carna went to her father, and her father gave her a beautiful piece of tanned leather as big as a bull, for it was the skin of the brown bull. Her father said, "Before you do anything else, go to the white cow in the pasture, and tell her you are sorry to take her son. Tell her he will travel the world." And he smiled at Carna, and Carna smiled back, for she realized that she would see the world too. Carna went to the pasture and found the white cow, her head bowed to the ground, pulling tufts of thick green grass. The air smelled of spring and the wet earth.

"I'm taking the skin of the brown bull to the cobbler for my boots. I am sorry," Carna said. The white cow raised her head and looked at Carna with her enormous eyes and let out a long, low sigh. In the sigh Carna heard the white cow say, "Yes, now you may go."

Carna walked through the town until she came to the cobbler's house. She knocked on the front door, and the cobbler answered. She said she was her mother's daughter and held up the skin. Before she could speak to ask for boots, the cobbler held up his hand to stop her and let Carna

The story of Carna began with the phrase "boots of seven strides," which came to me one morning while I was half-asleep. I'd been reading Richard Kennedy's stories and thinking about a friend's lament over the lack of strong mothers and women in stories. All of that played a part in the tale's germination.

123

through his house, through the front room and kitchen, into his shop. Boots and shoes and pieces of leather crowded around him, filling up the room. The cobbler held the leather up to the light. "This is a fine piece of leather," he said.

He looked down at Carna's feet and up at her again. "How many strides in these boots?"

"Seven," Carna said.

"Seven is a good number," he said. "Come back in three days, and you will have your boots of seven strides."

When Carna returned to the cobbler's house in three days, the cobbler brought her in, and she found her boots sitting by the fireplace in the front room. They were the color of butterscotch. They were enormous. But when she put them on, they seemed to fit—at least, until she tried to walk across the room, and then she stumbled and fell to her knees.

"Ah," said the cobbler. "You need to learn to walk again." And so Carna took off the boots and carried them home. She showed them to her mother, and there, sitting on the ground amid the rows of flowers in the garden, her mother said, "Put them on." Carna did, and her mother said, "Never put these boots on unless you know where you are going. If you don't know where you are going, anywhere is fine, and you don't need them. When you put them on, you must say where you want to go, and you must speak these words," and Carna's mother said in a soft singing voice:

> One stride for each direction, the south, east, west, and north,
> One stride for the earth that brought the living forth,
> One stride for the sky, the moon and sun o'erhead,
> And one to bring me home again to sleep in my own bed.

She made Carna repeat the words over and over again until she

124

learned them by heart. And when her mother was satisfied that Carna knew the words, she asked, "Now where do you want to go?"

"Well," said Carna, "How about the front gate?"

"Then it's to the gate with you. Go."

And in seven steps, seven strides, Carna walked across the yard and to the gate. Then she turned and came back. In seven strides.

"Where next?" asked her mother.

"To the well." And in seven strides Carna walked across the yard, behind the barn, to the well. Once again she walked back. "This time, to the oak tree on the other side of the field," she said, a smile spreading across her face as her mother watched. Once again, in seven steps, she crossed the open meadow to the oak tree and back.

"Now," said her mother, "You have your boots of seven strides."

For the next week Carna practiced—each time saying the rhyme, saying where she wanted to go, and reaching her destination in seven strides. Further and further she went each day, until one day she came to her parents and said, "It's time for me to leave home."

Her father simply nodded, as if he had been expecting it. Her mother rose and went to the kitchen. She returned with a wineskin and held it out to Carna. She said, "This is the milk of the white cow. Take it with you on your journey; it will keep. When you have gone as far as you will go, take this and give it away. And then come back home."

Carna placed the skin in her pack, and the next morning she put on her boots and stood in her yard, with her parents at the door. She said:

> *One stride for each direction, the south, east, west, and north,*
> *One stride for the earth that brought the living forth,*
> *One stride for the sky, the moon and sun o'erhead,*
> *And one to bring me home again to sleep in my own bed.*

She looked at her parents, waved, and said, "Take me to the next village." And she began her journey that day with seven steps to the next village. In the days that followed she traveled on, until one morning she stood high on the hills that she had once seen in the distance from her parents' house. Her homeland stretched out before her, already far away. Then she turned and continued over the hills to the next country.

For weeks and months Carna traveled on, each day awakening, deciding where she wanted to go, reciting the rhyme, and traveling there in seven strides. Sometimes Carna slept at an inn, sometimes at the house of someone she had met along the way, and sometimes out under the stars. As she traveled, stories about her spread: stories of a girl in large boots who walked with the wind. Some said they had seen her, traveling by them on a day when she was going only a short distance. But some said they only felt her go by, for on the days she traveled great distances, people noticed only the breeze she created as she walked by them.

One night Carna stayed at an inn and shared a meal with some other travelers. After the dinner they sat back in their chairs and traded stories of their journeys. At last, when it had grown silent, one man who had been quiet spoke softly. "Ah, but the country I've been to, I've never seen another like it," he said. "For in that country lives a giant, a huge creature with three eyes: two in the front and one in the back. And the one in the back is terrible—it never closes. So you can't come up from behind the giant, for he always sees you. He comes out at night and stalks the roads and countryside. One night I heard him roaring and bellowing as he passed by where I was staying. Why, the whole earth shook."

Another traveler said, "I've been to that country, but I left as soon as I could. It's a sad thing to see a whole race of people so terrified."

Carna asked, "What does the giant do? Does he eat people or destroy villages? What will he do if he finds people outside?"

Both men shook their heads, and the first answered, "I don't know.

No one I met had ever known of a person's being caught. You see, they all run inside and lock their doors at night. And none go out till the light of the morning."

"And where is this place?" asked Carna.

"Far to the east," he said, "over the mountains that look like clouds on the horizon."

The second man answered, "Yes, it's so far that it seems to be not in this world but another." A breeze blew through the window by the table. The candle flickered, and the room was filled with the smell of lilacs and early summer. Carna knew where she wanted to go.

The next morning, up with the sun, Carna had a breakfast and, wearing her boots of seven strides, stood outside the door of the inn and spoke the rhyme. "Take me to the mountains in the East," she called out. And that day, in seven long strides, moving more swiftly and surely than she had ever traveled before, she walked toward the mountains. As she went, she saw the mountains grow larger and larger, rising to meet her. And on the seventh step that day, as the sun set behind her, she reached the foot of the great mountains. As the night fell, the mountains turned dark above her, except for their tops, blanketed with snow, which shone like a silver fire in the moonlight.

The next morning she arose and headed over the mountains. She could feel the air growing colder and colder as she climbed higher. She looked below her and saw eagles circling on the wind, which howled through the canyons. On the fourth step, as she crossed over the peaks, she looked down and saw a long green valley stretched before her, sprinkled with villages and farms, forests and roads. On her seventh step that day she reached the valley and found herself in a grove of tall pines. She was in the land of the giant.

When she awoke the next morning, Carna did not put on her boots because she didn't know where she was going. She walked until she came to a village, and when she came across a man walking the other way, she stopped him. "Excuse me," she said, "but could you tell me about the giant who lives in this country?" The man's eyes grew wide, and his brow creased, and instead of answering, he walked by her at a hurried pace. She asked the same question of the next person she met, but this woman only turned from her and ran inside her house.

Wherever she went, she received the same response. It seemed to her that the country and people had no soul, or that the heart of the land was hidden from view, for fear that it would be taken. She walked through village after village, and everywhere she went, she was greeted in the same manner, until she came to the city at the center of the kingdom, and there at the center of the city was the castle of the king and queen. Carna reached the castle and pounded upon the door. A guard answered her. "State your business," he said.

"I've come to see the king and queen about the giant. It's important."

Carna was ushered into the throne room. Carna could see the king and queen seated at the end of the great room. She walked toward them.

The king spoke. "Where is the person who wished to speak to us about the giant?"

"It is I," said Carna.

The queen called out, "But this is a mere girl. What does she know? What can she do?"

The king said angrily, "Do not insult us. Guard, take her away. Now!"

The guard grabbed Carna by the collar and pulled her across the room and through the halls of the castle, until she was shoved out the back door. The door slammed and locked behind her. Carna sat on the curb of the street by the back of the castle and watched the sun set behind the houses of the city. The people moved silently about, attending to their business. But when the clock in the castle tower struck seven, the people hurried to their houses, scurrying like small animals. Carna could hear the doors being barred and saw the shades being drawn tight so there was no light to be seen in the city. As the sky grew darker and the stars came out, Carna sat alone in the streets of that city, far from home, and wondered what she should do.

Then she felt the earth rumble beneath her, with a rhythmic shaking that grew stronger and stronger, until she could hear the sound of foot-steps, which shook even the walls of the castle. Carna raised her head and looked up, and off in the distance, coming closer and closer, she could see a dark shadow sweeping toward the city. As it came nearer, she heard a roaring and bellowing along with the footsteps. It was the giant. Closer and closer he came, until he reached the edge of the city, and there, when he came to a small hill, the giant sat down upon it, put his head in his hands, and moaned with a long, mournful sound.

Carna reached into her pack and pulled out her boots of seven strides. Reciting the rhyme, she said, "Take me to the giant." And in seven quick strides she went through the streets of the city to its edge, reaching the hill. There she stopped, standing before the giant, a rough and weathered creature, and called to him.

The giant raised his head from his hands and saw the girl standing before him. His brow furrowed. "How did you get here?" he said brusquely. "You could not have come from behind me."

Carna shrugged, even though her heart beat so loudly that to her it sounded as loud as the giant's footsteps. She answered, "It doesn't matter how I've come, only that I'm here."

The giant persisted, "But I see everything. I can see at night, and I see those trying to move behind me and fool me; I see them, and they cannot trick me. I don't trust them. I see them."

Carna said, "Your eye behind is powerful."

A change came over the giant's face. He held his head in his hands and looked up again. "A power is a curse," he answered. "For the eye never closes, so I cannot sleep. That is why I walk the roads at night."

Carna looked up at the giant and realized something that no one else had: the giant was miserable. "Then," she said, "the eye must come out." Before the giant knew what was happening, Carna had called out the rhyme and said, "Take me to the top of the giant." She began climbing up the side of the seated giant—up his leg, to his waist, onto his back, climbing and pulling until she reached his hair, which hung down below his shoulders. Carna began to pull herself up by the giant's hair. Roaring, the giant reached back with both hands, trying to grab hold of Carna, and swung his head back and forth, trying to shake her loose. But Carna was quick and strong, and she held on, climbing until she came to the back of the giant's head.

There, holding on with one hand, she reached up to the giant's third eye with her free hand and pulled and pulled and pulled until it came free and fell to the ground. Holding on to the giant's hair, swinging back and forth high above the ground, Carna realized that she had gone as far as she would ever go and remembered her mother's words. With one hand she reached back into her pack and pulled out the skin that held the white cow's milk. She poured the milk into the eyeless socket, and the wound healed instantly, leaving only a faint pink scar. The giant calmed and became silent.

Carna swung down on the giant's hair to his shoulder. The giant looked down at Carna, feeling behind his head. "My eye . . . I can't see. What is behind me? What is there? I can't see. What is behind me?"

Carna looked up at the giant's enormous, bewildered face and answered, "Nothing but your fears."

Then the giant lay down upon that small hill and fell asleep. Carna climbed down and walked across the road to where the eye lay, dull and lifeless. She knelt down, picked it up, and put it into her pack.

The next morning people found the giant sleeping at the edge of town.

They stood at a great distance from him when they saw him waking. But after a while they saw that he was not dangerous and came closer. In time one of the townspeople crawled into the giant's hand, and although the giant could have crushed out the man's life, he did not.

Carna was called to the castle, and there she explained what had happened. The king and queen stood up from their thrones, knelt before Carna, and apologized for their rudeness. "Stay," said the king, "and I will make you Protector of the Kingdom."

"No," Carna answered. "Ask the giant. He will be your protector. It is time for me to go home." Carna walked out of the throne room. Servants and others lined the halls as she reached the castle doors. Outside a huge crowd parted as Carna walked into the street. There she put on her boots of seven strides, spoke the rhyme, and said, "Take me home."

Over seven days and nights, around the rest of the world, Carna traveled homeward. On the fourth night, as she crossed the deepest ocean, she opened her sack and let the eye of the giant drop into the black waters. At the end of her seventh step, she reached home, and in the garden she found her mother, who to Carna's eyes somehow seemed older and softer—not quite so large and strong as before. When Carna emptied her sack in the garden, it held only seeds and earth from around the world. Carna's mother picked up the seeds and carried them to her garden, where she planted them.

Carna built her own house close to her parents' home, and in it she set a huge fireplace. When all was finished, she built a large fire on the hearth, took off the boots of seven strides, and left them there by the fire. And if Carna is still there, so are the boots of seven strides.

Bill Harley of Seekonk, Massachusetts, studied religion in college, then began a full-time career as a musician and a storyteller. An award-winning recording artist and performer, Harley is best known for his work with family audiences.

THE DAY THE COW ATE MY BRITCHES

Ray Hicks

When I was growin' up, all the entertainment we'd have was tellin' stories. When us youngun's would git together, and we'd git a little rough, somebody would start one of them tales, and all of us kids would quiet down. You could hear a pin drop. Tellin' tales is natural for me. Do you want to hear about the time the cow ate my britches?

There was a family of Indians that lived way down in the holler. And they had a little girl, and I loved 'er. If I could jist hear her voice, it would make me feel good. So finally one fall, 'long about the last of October or the first o' November, I begged my mama to let me go down to see 'er.

I had no shoes, and I had to go barefooted, but my feet were so crusty and tough that I could crack chestnuts with my heels. And my mama had made me a little ol' pair of britches with a little blouse that hung over 'em.

Mama didn't want me to go, but she said, "You're a-goin' to go or die, ain't ye?"

I said, "It's a-killin' me. I've got to see that little girl and hear 'er talk."

So she said, "You ain't a-goin' to let me alone, so go on."

I took off down the holler and soon got there, a-wearin' this little ol' blouse and my little britches.

The little girl was bashful. She'd sit over in one corner of their old log cabin, head down, with her hand over her face, and maybe she'd giggle a little, now and then, you know, and peep out when her mother wasn't lookin'.

Directly, it started snowin'—them was the purtiest snowflakes—and I thought I'd better hit it home. But her mother said, "Wait till my husband comes in, and see what he says."

So directly, he come in. He was probably out choppin' wood for that old mud fireplace, and it was a-gittin' purty late.

And she said, "This little Hicks boy is a-wantin' to take off in this storm. He's bare-footed and a-wearin' jist these little ol' short britches with a little blouse. He might die. And we love 'im."

And the husband said, "No, son, you can't go. You'll have to stay with us now."

So we sat down there at that old fireplace, and they got to tellin' Jack tales and ghost tales and stories about the Indians. And I loved listenin' to

132

them tales.

Directly, it was time to retire, and they put me in a little ol' bunk 'side the wall. I was a-layin' there, and the mud had fell out between those logs right where my head was a-layin', and, God, I hated to name it to 'em, but snow was a-pepperin' in on my face, and I knew I wouldn't live till mornin'. So I happened to think of my britches, and I stuffed 'em in the hole between the logs where the mud had fell out, and that fixed it.

The next morning I grabbed for my britches, and they was gone. An old cow outside that cabin had ate them up. I'd had it. There I was with no britches, only a-wearin' this little ol' blouse. I couldn't git outa bed, so I played off sick.

I told 'em, "I'm a little puny. I don't believe I can git up." So they went to brewin' up some medicine, and they made me drink a pint of that juice. I turned 'er up and got 'er down, and I thought to myself, *If nothin's wrong with me, that stuff's liable to kill me deader than the dickens.*

The daddy went off a-cuttin' wood, and the mama and the little girl went to milk the cow. Directly, while I was a-layin' there, they come in with the milk in a bucket and sat it down on a little table. They had forgot the strainer at the springhouse, so they took off to go to the spring. I didn't know how fer it was to the spring, but I thought I'd have time to git up and drink a little of that milk, even if it wasn't strained.

And so I was a-drinkin' it, a-lappin' it up dog-style, with my head down in the pail and with no britches on, and they came in on me. It startled me so bad that when I lifted my head up, I caught the handle of that bucket 'round my neck.

When I seen what I had done, I come to myself and made a dive for the bed. That milk, a little over half up, tilted me over, and I went under the bed and spilt the milk all over the floor. And then I made for the cabin door, and as I was leavin', I caught my foot in the handle of a slop bucket sittin' on the floor and drug it out the door.

It'd snowed two feet that night—some of the purtiest fluffy white snow I've ever seen—and I'd come home in that snow, a-runnin' as hard as I could and hadn't noticed that bucket hangin' 'round my neck. Mama said, "Where you been with your britches gone and that bucket 'round your neck?" I told her I'd got trapped. And you know, my daddy tried to make me take that bucket back. But there was one thing for sure: Ray wasn't gonna face 'em to take no bucket back. So my daddy took it back for me. I never did see that little girl no more, and, oh, God, what tales I could've learnt.

Ray Hicks, considered the patriarch of traditional storytelling in America, was named a National Heritage Fellow by the National Endowment for the Arts in 1983. Hicks, a farmer, lives in Banner Elk, North Carolina.

POSSUM, TURTLE, AND THE WOLVES

Doug Elliott

Possum is sort of a slow critter, not fast like a rabbit. He just ambles along, looking for things to eat, making a living as best he can. He can climb a tree but not quickly like a squirrel. He climbs slowly and carefully as you or I might.

Possum had a friend who was even slower than he was. His name was Turtle. Bright and early one morning, Possum said, "Come on, Brother Turtle, I want to take you out to my favorite tree." So he and Turtle ambled on over to a big persimmon tree. The tree was loaded with persimmons, and they looked very ripe. They were a rich orange color, and their skins were soft and wrinkly. Possum carefully tasted one of them. They didn't have any of the mouth-drying puckery taste than unripe persimmons are famous for. They were as soft and sweet as sugar plums.

Turtle said in his slow deep voice, "Well, they look pretty good, Brother Possum, but how am I gonna get some? I can't climb a tree."

"Don't worry, Brother Turtle," Possum said as he started up that tree. "I'll climb up and throw some down to you."

He got up in the tree, climbed out on a limb, and started eating some of the persimmons and tossing others down to Turtle. He'd eat one and toss one down, then he'd eat another and toss another down to Turtle. They felt like they were having a picnic.

"Keep 'em coming, Brother Possum," Turtle shouted (as well as he could with a mouthful of persimmon). "They sure are good!"

Possum continued throwing them down, and the two friends were having a wonderful time of it until all of a sudden, out of the bushes came a great big wolf. Now, Possum knew he was up in the tree, where the wolf couldn't get him. Turtle knew that he could pull into his hard shell, where the wolf couldn't get him. But that wolf still ruined the picnic by standing right over Turtle and catching and eating all the persimmons that Possum was trying to throw down to Turtle. Possum threw them all around, thinking the wolf would miss some, but that wolf jumped up and caught them

The core of this story was collected in the late 1800s from a Cherokee Indian elder, and it is believed that some of the tale's elements may be African in origin. It's clear that over the past several centuries this story has been passed back and forth between cultures. The tale that comes down to us today is a rich one with universal appeal.

135

all before they even hit the ground. So Possum tried throwing the persimmons down very fast, one after the other, in rapid succession, but the wolf still managed to catch every one.

Possum didn't know what to do. That wolf might never leave them alone! Then he looked up higher in the tree, and there he saw a huge persimmon that was almost as big as a grapefruit. And that gave him an idea. First he started throwing down the small persimmons as fast as he could. That greedy old wolf had his jaws open wide so he could catch every one. When Wolf's jaws were flapped open as wide as they could be, Possum heaved down the giant persimmon as hard as he could, and the wolf caught it right in the throat. That persimmon stuck there, and the wolf soon keeled over dead. As Possum climbed down the tree, Turtle remarked in his slow deep voice, "That sure was good thinking, Brother Possum. I didn't think that wolf would ever leave us alone."

They stood for a moment and looked at the big dead wolf. Then Turtle said, "I didn't tell you, Brother Possum, but I'm about to go on a long journey, and the one thing I need for my traveling bag is a couple of spoons. Then if somebody offers me a meal along the way, I could use the spoons to eat with, and I could also use them for ladling water out of streams when I get thirsty."

"What has that got to do with a dead wolf?" Possum asked.

Turtle replied, "I just figured out where I'm gonna get those spoons. I'm gonna cut that wolf's ears off and make wolf-ear spoons." And that's just what Turtle did. He cut those ears off, took them over to the stream, scrubbed them out, and laid them on the rocks to dry in the morning sun.

As the sun shone down, those ears dried out, and as they dried, they curled up. It wasn't long before they looked a lot like spoons.

When the ears were all dried out, Turtle tucked them into his traveling kit and started down the trail. "See you later, Brother Possum. Thanks for that delicious 'simmon breakfast." And down the trail he went, just a-walking and a-hiking and a-walking and a-hiking. And for a turtle, he traveled quite far that morning.

As the noon hour approached, he started to get hungry, but he couldn't find anything to eat. There weren't any persimmon trees, and even if there had been, his possum buddy wasn't there to climb them for him. There were no berries or worms or snails or anything else that turtles like to eat. So he just kept on a-walking and a-hiking, getting hungrier all the time.

Soon he came to a village, and as he walked by, some people came out and said, "Hey there, Turtle! It looks like you've been traveling. Do you want something to eat?" Turtle said that, indeed, he was hungry, so the people invited him into a lodge to have a bowl of hominy.

They put the hominy in front of him and said, "Now just a minute, Turtle. We'll get you a spoon, and you can have all you want." Turtle replied, "That's all right, I've got my own spoon, thanks." And he reached into his traveling bag, pulled out one of his wolf-ear spoons, and started eating that hominy. Nobody thought anything about it at first, until someone noticed what Turtle was eating with. They started whispering among themselves, "What's that turtle eating with?"

"It looks like a wolf's ear!"

"A wolf's ear! Where would a turtle get a wolf's ear?"

"Could he have killed a wolf? I didn't think a turtle could kill a wolf!"

Right then, somebody came into the lodge and heard just the last part of the whispered conversation. "Killed a wolf? Who killed a wolf? That turtle kills wolves? I'm getting out of here!" Soon the rumor was spreading through the village like wildfire. "There's a wolf-killing turtle on the loose, and he's right here in our village!" Those foolish people were thrown into a panic, and they all ran to the woods, hid in the bushes, crawled into hollow logs, or climbed up in trees.

Turtle continued eating his hominy. He didn't know why everybody had disappeared so fast. When he finished, he crawled out of the lodge and looked around. There was no one in sight, so he called out, "So long, folks. I'll be on my way now. Thanks for the meal." And down the trail he went, a-walking and a-hiking and a-walking and a-hiking.

In the meantime, all the people came back to the village and congratulated one another for their quick escape from the dangerous wolf-killing turtle. Everybody was talking about it. Every boy told every girl, every girl told every mama, every mama told every dad, every dad told every grandpa, told every grandma, told every dog, told every cat, told every mouse, told every rat, told every frog, told every bird, told every squirrel, told every rabbit, told every fox, told every snake, told every bug, and soon the forest was buzzing with the rumor of the wolf-killing turtle. Turtle didn't know a thing about it—he just continued slowly and steadily down the trail, just a-walking and a-hiking.

He traveled along for several more hours, and the sun was beating down. He was getting very thirsty, but he couldn't find any water to drink: not a spring or a stream or even a puddle. He came to another village, and as he approached, some people came out and said, "Hey there, Turtle; it sure is hot today. Aren't you thirsty?"

"I sure am," said Turtle.

"Well, come on over. We just made some fresh sumac lemonade. It's right here in this pot. We'll get you a ladle, and you can scoop out all you want."

"Oh, that's all right," said Turtle, "I've got my own little ladle right here." And he reached into his traveling bag, pulled out one of the wolf ears, and started slurping away. Nobody thought anything of it until they noticed what Turtle was using for a ladle.

Now, we all know that turtles travel pretty slowly. However, rumors travel a whole lot faster, and would you believe that the rumor about the wolf-killing turtle had gotten to this village long before Turtle himself had arrived? Of course, everybody figured it was just a silly rumor, and nobody believed it, because how could a little turtle kill a great big wolf anyway? It just couldn't be true.

But when they saw Turtle pull out that wolf's ear, they knew that the rumor must be true, and in an instant this village too was thrown into panic and fear. Soon everybody was running to the woods, climbing up trees, hiding in the bushes, or crawling into hollow logs.

Turtle kept on slowly slurping away at the sumac drink. When he stopped and looked around, he noticed that everyone was gone. "Now, what got into them?" he said to himself. "This bunch of humans is even stranger than the people I met in that last village." He drank his fill of the tangy juice and felt very refreshed. "Thanks for the drink, folks, wherever you are," he shouted over his shoulder as he started down the trail, a-walking and a-hiking.

Before too long the people came out of hiding and started talking excitedly among themselves, and soon the rumor of the wolf-killing turtle had spread to every corner of the forest. Turtle just kept trudging slowly along. He didn't know anything about the rumors that were being spread about him. But he did notice something peculiar as he traveled. He would hear the birds singing and the squirrels and chipmunks scurrying around ahead of him on the trail, but as he got closer to them, the woods would become absolutely quiet. All the critters were hiding because they had heard about the wolf-killing turtle, and they were afraid that he might kill them too.

It made Turtle uneasy not to hear all the other animals around him as he walked, especially as he neared a thick dark place in the woods. He just kept on slowly, a-walking and a-hiking. Suddenly, out of the bushes came a whole pack of wolves, and they surrounded him. Everywhere he looked, all he could see was growling wolves and sharp teeth. He blinked and said, "Uh oh . . ."

The leader of the pack swaggered up. "All right, Turtle," he snarled. "So you're the one who's been killing our brothers!" And he reached into Turtle's traveling bag and pulled out the wolf-ear spoons. He held the ears up to the other wolves and howled in rage. "Look, Brothers, what more proof do we need? This is the wolf-killer, all right!"

"But . . . but," Turtle protested.

"No buts about it," the wolf leader rudely interrupted. "We're gonna put a stop to this wolf-killing right here and now."

"Let's build a fire," one of the wolves suggested, "and throw him in it and burn him up. What do you think of that, Turtle?"

Turtle knew what to say. "Well, you just go ahead and throw me in that fire. I wouldn't mind at all. No sir, I'd just roll around in that fire with my hard shell and put your fire right out."

The wolves muttered among themselves, "We'd better think of something worse than that." Then one of them barked, "I know—let's get a big clay pot of water. We'll put him in it, build a big fire under it, and boil him."

Turtle said, "Go ahead and try to boil me. I wouldn't mind that at all. I'd just kick around in that old pot and hit it with my hard shell, and it would crack your pot. Then the water would come out and drown your fire—and you'd have a broken pot besides."

The wolves began talking among themselves, trying their best to think of something worse, when one of them said, "I know, let's take him to the river. We'll throw him in, and he'll drown!"

Turtle thought to himself, *I wouldn't mind that. I'm a good swimmer.* But he was a smart turtle, and this is what he said. "No! Don't throw me in the river. That would be the worst thing you could do! Burn me or boil me, if you must, but please, oh please, don't throw me in the river!"

Those foolish wolves said, "If that's the worst thing we can do, let's do it." And they marched Turtle straight to a river bank high up over the water. One of those wolves grabbed his front legs, and another grabbed his back legs, and they started swinging him. One, two, three! They threw him off the river bank.

Turtle sailed through the air, end over end, down toward the river, until—wham!—he hit a rock and splashed into the water. When he felt the cool water all around him, he knew that all he had to do was swim across the river, and he would be home free. But as soon as he began to swim his first stroke, he felt a sharp pain. "Oh, my aching back," he moaned.

He had really hurt his back when he hit that rock. In fact, he could hardly swim at all, so he ended up having to half-swim and half-limp. Slowly, slowly he made his way across the river. When he reached the other side, he found a sloping sandbar that was overhung with wild plants and bushes. He pulled himself up on the sandbar and crawled up under the bushes to rest.

His back hurt so badly that he didn't even want to look at it. But he knew he had to, and when he finally did look, he saw that his shell was all cracked and broken. He didn't know what to do. Then he noticed some of the plants that were growing around him. They were medicinal herbs: mint and willow and comfrey and even backache root. Turtle sniffed the mint, chewed the willow bark, and rubbed the comfrey and the backache root all over his sore, broken shell.

That night he sang medicine songs and prayed to the Great Spirit, and soon he was fast asleep. The next morning when he woke, he felt much better, and when he looked back over his shell, all the pieces had come back together, and the cracks had healed. And to this day you can still see the cracks in Turtle's shell.

Doug Elliott is a storyteller, a naturalist, a herbalist, and a back-country guide. The author of several books of stories and woods lore, Elliott lives in Union Mills, North Carolina.

BLACK HAIR

Brenda Wong Aoki

This story has haunted me for years. When I researched its origins, I found that it came from one of the oldest collections of Japanese mythology. There is a Japanese phrase, mono no aware, *that means "the poignant beauty of the fleetingness of life." This tale has that kind of feel to it—something that lingers in the air.*

Mukashi, *mukashi*—long, long time ago—there lived in Kyoto a samurai who was reduced to poverty by the ruin of his lord. The samurai had the good fortune to be married to a kind and beautiful wife with clear fair skin, soft brown eyes, and long luxurious hair—blue-black as the night, shining as the stars, and soft as a cloud.

Day after day the samurai sat drowning his sorrows in his sake cup, while day after day his good wife went to the market to sell her jeweled hair ornaments, her silken gowns. The samurai never noticed how she often went hungry so that he could eat his fill. He only sat drowning his sorrows in his sake cup.

One day the samurai looked up. "Hmph!" he said, sulking. "I lose everything, and now I lose all face by wearing rags. How I wish I had a new kimono."

The next day the samurai awoke at noon as usual and was just about to begin drinking his sake, when he heard *Zu ka, zu ka, zu ka*. Curious, he got up and followed the sound, until he came to the little room where his wife was working. Sliding open the paper door, he saw her there, with her hair cut as short as a little boy's, weaving her long silken tresses into cloth from which to make him a kimono.

Day after day she wove, never stopping to eat or sleep, until one day, pale and worn, she came out of the little room, carrying the most wonderful kimono—blue-black as the night, shining as the stars, and soft as a cloud. This she gave to the samurai.

"What kind of kimono is this?" he roared. "It has no crest on it. What kind of samurai would I be with no crest?"

Trembling with fear, his good wife answered, "My love, we are without a master. We have no crest."

"Then make one up!" said the samurai, with one hand raised to strike her. "Make me a symbol of great power."

So his good wife took the kimono back into her room. She had no money with which to buy dye or thread, so she bit her little finger until the blood ran crimson. Then in the most exquisite hand, she wrote in blood the symbol for *kokoro*: heart. This she gave to the samurai.

"Why have you written this on my kimono?" snarled the samurai, his black eyes hard and cold.

"You asked for a symbol of great power. The greatest power in all the world is that of a good heart," answered his good wife.

"Hmph!" said the samurai. Nevertheless, he was very pleased. You see, he thought that the crest written in blood made him look very brave. He went out into the street to show himself off. As he was strutting up and down the street, he chanced upon a magnificent procession, with 150 banner-men waving purple banners, followed by 300 samurai in full armor. At the center of the procession, on a white stallion bedecked with gold and jewels, sat a fair maid with long beautiful hair, almost as beautiful as his wife's had been, laughing eyes, and sharp white teeth.

"My, how handsome you look in that new kimono," purred the fair maid.

"I was just taking a break from my official duties," boasted the samurai.

"Ah," said the fair maid, "Not only are you very handsome, but you're also official. My father can use a man like yourself. My father is the Lord of Nagoya. Come with me. Show him your worth."

The samurai bowed thrice, raced back to his poor house, where his wife waited, and roared, "Draw me a bath, and help me look my best. I now have an important position with the Lord of Nagoya. I am to leave immediately."

His good wife was heartbroken. Nagoya is far from Kyoto. But she hid her tears in her threadbare sleeves and did as he asked.

When the samurai was dressed, he looked at her and said, "I'm not coming back till your hair grows out. You look like a boy!" And he was gone, just like that.

The samurai soon became a high official with the Lord of Nagoya, and the maid of Nagoya persuaded him to marry her. Now, a man cannot have two wives, so he sent a messenger to Kyoto, telling his good wife he had divorced her. The date was the 10th day of the ninth moon.

He married the maid, but wealth does not make one rich. His new wife proved to have a bad temper. She was quick to anger—quick to flash those sharp white teeth. She cared neither for his happiness nor his peace of mind. She cared only about new jeweled hair ornaments, sweet rice cakes, and "Come to bed now, my little official." And every night she hissed, "Show me your worth." The samurai was not happy.

Months passed, years passed. The samurai's new wife had long since lost the glow of youth—deep lines of boredom and disdain were etched into her face. These she hid with a thick white powder. Her lips were kept red only by a paint they call beni. Her body was plump with rice cakes. The only thing that remained of her former beauty was her sharp white teeth. "Show me your worth!" The samurai was miserable.

One night as he lay in his bed unable to sleep, he heard *Zu ka, zu ka, zu ka*. Was it a servant passing in the night? Suddenly, as though with the wave of a great tsunami, he was overcome with yearning for his good wife. He remembered her kind, gentle ways. Then he remembered the kimono. Made of her own hair. Emblazoned with a crest written in her blood!

The samurai searched for that kimono. Finally, in a room filled with things long since forgotten, he found the kimono—blue-black as the night, shining as the stars, and soft as a cloud. As if in a dream, he heard her say, "This is for you, my love, because the greatest power in all the world is that of a good heart."

The samurai decided then and there to go back to his good wife. He marched into his second wife's chambers and divorced her on the spot.

"You married me for my money," she cried, "and now that you have it and I'm old and ugly, you leave me."

"Save your mouth for rice cakes," he said. And he was gone, just like that.

Clad only in the blue-black kimono and riding his fastest stallion, the samurai raced back to Kyoto. The journey was hard. The road had changed. He was no longer a young man. Twenty years had passed since he'd last been that way. He reached Kyoto at nightfall.

The moonlight made everything visible. Following the crooked streets, he came to the little alley where he had once lived. He found the house quite easily, but it had a different look. It was not the poor but tidy house he remembered. Tall weeds were growing on the roof. The date was the 10th day of the ninth moon.

He knocked on the front door. When no one answered, he slid it open and stepped inside. The front room was empty . . . matless. A chilly wind blew through the holes in the floor. The moon shone through tears in the paper walls. The house looked completely abandoned. Still the samurai was determined to search each and every room. Finally, he came to the little room that had been his wife's favorite resting place. Noticing a glow within, he approached the door.

Sliding open the paper door, he saw her there. She had not changed in 20 years! Her skin was clear and fair, her eyes soft and brown, and her hair had grown back again—blue-black as the night, shining as the stars, and soft as a cloud.

She looked at him, saying only, "My love, how glad I am to have you back, if only for a moment."

"Only for a moment?" sobbed the samurai. "For all eternity. I am a rich man now. Tomorrow I send for my servants and all my money. You'll never have to suffer again."

She looked at him and smiled. That night in what once had been their bridal chamber, they lay down to rest. Reaching out over 20 years, their bodies joined as one.

When the samurai awoke, sunlight was streaming through the tears in the paper walls. But he found to his amazement that he was not lying on a soft bed but on a moldy, rotten floor. Was it a dream? No. There she lay. She was sleeping. He bent to kiss that dear cheek.

"Augh!" The sleeper had no face. Beside him lay the corpse of a woman, a corpse so decayed that little remained but bones crawling with insects, and long, tangled black hair. Screaming and screaming, the samurai ran into the street, bumping into an old man. "What's wrong?" asked the old man. Unable to speak, the samurai pointed to the house.

"But no one lives there. That house belonged to the wife of a samurai who left her to marry another. Heart-broken, she grew sick. She died on the 10th day of the ninth moon . . . 20 years ago."

Brenda Wong Aoki's unique storytelling presentations blend song, dance, and drama. A student of Japanese classical theater since 1979, she is well-known for her ghost and demon stories. Aoki lives in San Francisco.

THE PINCH-HITTER

Michael Parent

By late August of my 13th year, I'd had my Social Security card for more than three years, won the junior checkers championship at the neighborhood playground twice, and ridden my bike the seven miles to Martin's Point Beach a few times. But I'd never once gotten a base hit off Billy Boudreau.

School was about to start again in a few days. So if I didn't do it real soon, I'd probably have to wait until next year. I'd spend the whole endless winter watching my friends play that other game, the one all of us Canuck kids in Lewiston, Maine, were supposed to be good at and that I had barely begun to play 'cause I couldn't skate very well. And I'd have to take crap from Pete Poliquin, who'd never even touched one of Billy's fastballs but didn't seem to care about it like I did. I'd see Billy around in the winter, but he never said anything. Nobody could hit him, and he wasn't the bragging type anyway. All the other pitchers at the neighborhood ball field threw fastballs that looked like grapefruits, while Billy threw Bayer aspirins, but he never pointed that out. He didn't have to.

We gathered early on what I hoped would be The Day. We wanted to squeeze in as many innings as we could, and soon we had enough guys for two teams. Billy and Jake Houle, the two best players, did the choosing up. Jake tossed a bat to Billy, who caught it upside-down on the thick end, and then they went hand-above-hand up the bat until Jake capped the knob with his thumb. First pick. I was a pretty good fielder, so I wasn't worried about getting picked last and exiled to right field. I just hoped Jake would pick me so I could hit against Billy as soon as possible.

"'Allo, les garcons, 'ow you're doing?" said Monsieur Gauthier. He and his chum Monsieur Caron sat at their usual spots along the third-base line. "Hey, I 'ope we're gonna see some better baseball today den we saw at Fenway over de weekend." They were retired from the mill and mostly watched and talked baseball. They'd stop by a few times each day, comment on our games, offer pointers, and move on.

My inspiration for "The Pinch-Hitter" was Alden Bigelow's "It Isn't Fair." But this tale is really a story about my godfather, Joseph Fournier, and my telling is a tribute to him. "The Pinch-Hitter" will be included in a collection of my stories to be published by Soleil Press.

Jake picked me to play first base since I could handle his strong throws from shortstop. By noon I'd made him look smart by digging some low ones out of the dirt and making the routine plays too. We broke for lunch. We'd played two games, Billy'd pitched in one, and I'd faced him four times, with the usual results: four strikeouts.

After lunch Monsieur Gauthier and Monsieur Caron came by again while Billy was pitching, which meant they'd stay longer than usual. Billy was mowing our batters down, barely pausing between pitches. He could pitch his end of a nine-inning game in about 27 minutes. The two baseball sages interrupted a conversation about Nap Lajoie, a Hall of Famer of French-Canadian descent, to take a closer look at Billy.

"'E can pitch, dat kid, einh?"

"Ah, oui—maybe 'e gonna t'row for de Sox one good day."

"Dose Sox need all de help we can give dem, einh?"

"You can say dat again! Yeah, 'e's got an arm on 'im, dat's for sure."

Billy stood relaxed on the mound, but he was all business up there. He kept to himself on and off the field. Guys knew he wouldn't stand for anyone but his mama to call him by his French name, Guillaume, and there was a rumor that he was a nephew of the great Indians shortstop Lou Boudreau. Beyond that, he was as elusive as his fastball.

The next batter was my buddy Pete Poliquin. Fastball, low and inside, swing and a miss. Fastball, belt-high across the heart of the plate, swing and a miss, strike two. Pete called timeout and stepped out of the batter's box. From the on-deck circle I noticed the kid we called the Phantom Kid leaning against the fence along the first-base line. Pete stepped back in. Billy fired a third pitch, right down the middle again. Pete took a big cut and fouled it off behind the backstop. Then he flung his bat like a baton twirler and strode away from home plate. "Pete, where ya goin'? You still got one more strike," I said. "That's it for me," he said. "I'm retirin'. Baseball ain't gonna get no better than this."

The game was way out of reach, 12–0, so it didn't matter much, but I wasn't going to pass up any chance to swing against Billy. I stepped to the plate and saw that the Phantom Kid had moved closer, eyeballing me as though he knew what an important at-bat this was. He usually leaned over by the far post that supported the elbow-high fence along the first-base grandstands. Now he was up near the home-plate end of the fence. He'd showed up after supper the last couple of weeks, appearing and disappearing without ever talking to anyone. We'd never asked him to play. I wondered how long he'd stay this time before he disappeared.

I focused on Billy again. This could be it. I tugged at my cap, pulled up my pants, tapped the bat on the plate, and spit into the other batter's box. Then—the final touch—I tapped the dirt out of my "spikes" like the pros did. It didn't matter that my spikes were really P.F. Flyers sneakers, so worn that the only dirt I'd tapped loose had been filling the center holes in the soles. I tried to gain that crucial mental edge by giving Billy a look that said, "C'mon, rookie, quit shakin', and fire your best pitch up here to ol' Ted Williams, Jackie Robinson, Yogi Berra, so I can smack it into the next county." It wasn't easy to hold that look, since by then Billy had struck me out 11 times. I was as ready as I could get for Billy's three aspirin tablets.

Then the Phantom Kid shouted, "Hey, can I pinch-hit?"

"You wanna pinch-hit for me?"

"Yeah, if it's okay."

"Well, I dunno, this is my last bat and I . . . "

"But you've been battin' all day," he said.

"Yeah, so what? Hey, what the hell's your name anyway?"

"Charlie. So whaddya think—can I pinch-hit?"

"What de hell, give 'im a try," Monsieur Caron called out. "''E can't do no worse den you guys."

"Damn!" I said under my breath. "Okay, okay. Here ya go." I held the bat out to the Phantom Kid. I figured he'd just strike out. But what if he got a hit with my at-bat? He paused a couple of seconds to reach behind the fence post, pulled a pair of crutches up under his arms, and came swinging out toward home plate.

Everyone watched him now as though he really were a phantom. The sun flashed on the metal braces clamped to his shoes. The kid swung the crutches out and pulled his legs along, but not like those people who get crutches because of a busted leg and usually start getting the hang of it right around the time the cast comes off.

Charlie stood in the lefties' batter's box. He bent down to adjust or maybe lock his leg braces, as I stood there holding the bat. He half-leaned on his crutches and grabbed the bat, and I stepped back toward the bench. Charlie looked out toward the pitcher's mound. He waved the bat in a slow circle like an old pro—or someone who's practiced with a mirror a lot—and waited for the pitch.

We waited. Billy picked up a handful of dirt, squeezed it, and threw it down, then stepped off the mound and back onto it. He took his glove off, wedged it under his arm, and rubbed the ball awhile without ever looking at the batter. No one told Billy to hustle it up. No one spoke at all. Billy's face was filled with a question he couldn't ask, and our eyes ping-ponged between Billy and Charlie. Even Monsieur Gauthier and Monsieur Caron made no comment.

We hadn't seen that look on Billy's face before. Charlie must have seen it someplace, though, because he's the one who finally answered Billy's question. "Hey, pitcher, it's okay. Just fire it in like you always do."

Billy shrugged, grinned at Charlie, eased into a slow windup, and threw a screaming fastball up to the plate—a perfect letter-high strike. It was the kind of pitch that's hard to see, let along hit. Every batter's dream is to swing perfectly into such a pitch and give it the kind of ride that outfielders must quickly admire before they chase it down.

And that's exactly what Charlie did. Pow! The ball sailed over Billy's astonished head and kept climbing. Richie Poirier, the center fielder, who had instinctively played Charlie quite shallow, scrambled after the ball as it sliced toward left-center field. "Look at dat, Henri! I be damn. Run, run like hell!" one of the men shouted.

Charlie was swinging, crutches and legs, down the first-base line—crutches and legs, crutches and legs. I couldn't believe it—his first time hitting against Billy. Damn! But soon I was up with the rest of the team, as we followed Charlie down the base path, screaming, "Go, Charlie, go!" and merging our will with his. The ball took just one bounce, about 15 feet away from a rusty sign that read 410, and settled at the base of the fence under the sign.

Charlie was halfway to first by the time Richie picked up the ball and turned to throw. Then Charlie got tangled up and fell forward, somehow managing to hang onto his crutches and fall hand-first. We all froze. You could see guys riffle through the rule books in their minds and then quickly put them aside to help Charlie up. But he waved them away, pushed himself back up, and kept crutching and legging down the line. Richie pegged a decent relay to Eugene at shortstop, and Eugene fired a one-hopper to first from shallow left-center field.

The screaming stopped, and the inning ended when the ball smacked into the first-baseman's glove and beat Charlie to the base by eight feet. If he'd been eight inches away, someone would have hollered, "Safe! Tie goes to the runner!" and heard no argument. But we knew that calling Charlie safe would have been the same as Billy's pitching him a slowball he didn't want.

Charlie returned to his spot by the post and watched from there. Billy Boudreau walked off the mound, shaking his head. The team behind him came in to bat as though they'd played badly, and we shuffled out to take the field, mouthing infield chatter that quickly faded into infield mumbles. All Monsieur Caron and Monsieur Gauthier could manage was a few whispers to each other. Charlie's turn at bat had filled the game with fiery mystery-juice, and now a hole had been punched into its bottom.

I didn't know what to think. I'd missed my last chance of the day and maybe of the season. The crippled kid who'd pinch-hit for me had practically made history but hadn't even made it to first base. When I finally looked over at Charlie, he was leaning on the fence at his usual spot with a huge smile on his face. What the hell was that about?

When the game ended, nobody said much, especially not to Charlie since no one had any idea what to say. I slipped my glove on the handle-bars of my skinny-wheel bike, hopped on the seat, and pointed it toward home. When the other guys left, I turned to Charlie. He was still smiling out to left-center field.

"Hey, Charlie, can I ask you somethin'?"

"Yeah, sure. Hey, what's your name?"

"The guys call me Bidou."

"Hey, thanks for lettin' me pinch-hit."

"Yeah. Listen, I was wonderin' what the heck you're so happy about after what happened."

"I played, man. I played," he said.

The street lights came on as I pedaled down Walnut Street. Rolling past the IGA Food Store, I wondered if Charlie had figured out how to ride a bike. I'd ask him next time. I carried my bike up the steps to our apartment, and I hoped Billy's fastball had even more steam on it when I faced him again, next week or next spring.

Michael Parent is a native Mainer of French-Canadian descent, now living in Charlottesville, Virginia. A former high school English teacher, Parent has performed traditional and original songs and stories since 1977.

Morgan and the Pot o' Brains

Milbre Burch

Morgan: *I put the sheep in the barn, Ma. The day's work is done.*

That's Morgan. He's a good-hearted lad, but he's not very smart. The people in his village call him a fool and a simpleton. But despite his simplicity, Morgan had plans for himself.

Morgan: *Ma, I've decided to visit the witch who lives on top of the hill. I'm going to ask her to sell me some brains. A whole pot of 'em. I'm going to get a pot o' brains.*
Mother: *That sounds like a good idea, Morgan. But don't forget to be polite to her. You've got to be polite to witches.*

So Morgan set out.

Morgan: *Do-te-do-do . . .*

He knocked once, twice, three times, then opened the door and gasped

> *Ah!*

The witch sat with her back to him, stirring something over the fire.

Morgan: *Good morning to you, missus.*
Witch: *Good morning to you, Morgan.*
Morgan: *She knows who I am without looking. That's pretty good . . . Uh . . . Nice weather we've been having.*
Witch: *Nice weather, Morgan, if you don't mind the rain.*
Morgan: *Well, now that we've both been so polite to each other, I've come to ask you if you'll sell me a pot o' brains.*
Witch: (Turning suddenly) *Oh, you did, did you? And did you want*

Years ago I discovered "Morgan and the Pot of Brains" in Ellen Pugh's Tales From the Welsh Hills. *Unable to resist the cleverness and charm of the story, I adapted it freely for telling. For me, Morgan uncovers the twin wisdoms of learning to ask for help when you need it and learning to depend on yourself.*

kings' brains or schoolmasters' brains?—'cause I don't have any of those to sell you.

Morgan: *No, ma'am, I just wanted plain brains. Like everybody's got. Or thinks they do.*

Witch: *Well, I might be able to help you. But you'll have to work for them.*

Morgan: *I don't mind working, missus.*

Witch: *I see that you don't. Then I want you to bring me the heart of the thing you love the best. And if it's the right thing, and you can answer a riddle, we'll see if we don't get you a pot of brains.*

Morgan: *Yes, missus, I'll be back.*

Morgan: *Ma, I saw the witch. She said to bring her the heart of the thing I love the best. Hmm. I don't know what that is. I love sunny days. I love green beans. I know, I'll take her the sheep's heart, Ma, 'cause I love to eat mutton best of all.*

Mother: *That sounds like a good idea, Morgan. It would be worth it if you come home with some brains, boy.*

So the next morning Morgan set out with the sheep's heart wrapped up in a cloth.

Morgan: (Triumphantly) *Oh-to-do-do, today's brains day. Missus, I brought you the heart of the thing I love the best. It's a sheep's heart.*

Witch: *I see that it is, Morgan. Let's see if it's the right thing then, boy. Here's your riddle: What runs without feet?*

Morgan: *Runs without feet? I don't know, missus.*

Witch: *Then you didn't bring the right thing, Morgan. Go on home, boy, but keep looking.*

Morgan: *Oh . . . all right, missus.*

But when Morgan got to his house, he saw that the neighbors had all gathered in the yard. And one of them came to him and said, "Morgan, come quick! Your mother's fallen ill, and we're afraid she's going to die."

Morgan: *Noooo!*

Morgan went inside, and sure enough, there was his mother lying on her bed. And when she saw him, she smiled as if to say, "I'm glad you've come home with some brains, boy, 'cause you're going to need them now." And then she did die.

Morgan: *Ma, oh, Ma, you shouldn't have left me. I loved you best of all! Oh! I hope this doesn't mean I have to take my mother's heart to the witch if I'm ever going to get my brains. Oh . . . maybe my whole mother would do.*

So he put her in a bag.

Morgan: (Sadly) *Missus, I brought you the heart of the thing I love the best.*
Witch: *I see that you did, Morgan. Let's see if it's the right thing, boy. Here's your riddle: What's yellow and shining and is not gold?*
Morgan: *Yellow and shining . . . yellow and shining . . . I don't know, missus!*
Witch: *Then you didn't bring the right thing, Morgan. Go on home, boy, but keep looking.*
Morgan: *Yes, missus.*

So Morgan picked up his burden and went out into the road. He lay the bag down beside a wall and started to cry his eyes out. But about that time a girl from the valley, a lass, came walking up the road. And when she saw this good-hearted boy crying fit to bust, something about him made her heart beat a little faster.

Lass: *Oh, what's the matter, boy?*

Morgan: (Sobbing) *Well, I killed my sheep . . . my mother's dead . . . and I don't have any brains. There's no one to take care of me . . .*

Lass: *Well . . . maybe I could . . . marry you and take care of you.*

Morgan: *You could? Can you cook?*

Lass: *I can cook real good.*

Morgan: *And can you sew and clean and mend?*

Lass: *I can do those things too.*

Morgan: *Well, then, I think you'll do.*

So they joined hands and went down to the village, and do you know that they were married and buried his mother all in the same afternoon? And they lived very happily for a time, until one day Morgan was working in the fields . . .

Morgan: *Oh! Lass! Lass! I came to tell you that I love you best of all.*

Lass: *That's nice to hear, Morgan, but did you have to stop your work to come to tell me that just now?*

Morgan: *You see, I was wondering if I have to kill you and take your heart up to the witch if I'm ever going to get my brains.*

Lass: *I bet you don't have to. Couldn't you take me with my heart beating nicely inside me the way that it is?*

Morgan: *Well, that might do. But then there's the riddles, and I never get the riddles right.*

Lass: *Maybe I could help you with the riddles.*

Morgan: *I don't know . . . Riddles is tough for womenfolk.*

Lass: *Why don't you try me?*

Morgan: *Well, there's one that goes, What runs without feet?*

Lass: *Water does.*

Morgan: *You're right. Well, what's yellow and shining and is not gold?*

Lass: *The sun is.*

Morgan: *Hey, you're good at this. Maybe we could do it.*

So they joined hands and went up to the witch's house. And they didn't have to knock this time, because she was sitting on her porch. And when she saw them coming together, she began to smile.

Morgan: *Good morning to you, missus. (Shyly) I brought you . . . the heart . . . of the thing I love the best.*

Witch: *I see that you did, Morgan. Let's see if it's the right thing, boy. Here's your riddle: What has always been there but is only a month old?*

Morgan: (Whispering) *I don't know the answer.*

Lass: (Whispering) *That would be the moon, Morgan.*

Morgan: *Ahem . . . that would be the moon, missus.*

Witch: *Aye, and you're right, Morgan. And I see you got yourself a pot of brains!*

Morgan: *Brains! I got brains! Uh . . . where are they, missus?*

Witch: *They're in your wife's head. You married 'em, Morgan.*

Morgan: *Well, so I did. And that's good!*

So Morgan and his wife joined hands and went back to their house, and they did live happily ever after. And Morgan never tried to buy a pot of brains again because his wife had enough to last them both a lifetime.

Milbre Burch, a student of acting and mime, creates lively characterizations and original dramatic monologues. She has been a professional storyteller since 1978 and lives in Pasadena, California.

THE INNKEEPER'S WISE DAUGHTER

Peninnah Schram

Whenever I tell this story, I think of my mother. Her father was not an innkeeper but a peddler of shoelaces in New York City's Lower East Side, a man who once owned a grocery store in the White Russian village of Lepl. In any case, she had the same marvelous women's logic shown by the innkeeper's wise daughter.

Many years ago in a small village in Russia, there were two friends—a tailor and an innkeeper. One day as they were drinking glasses of tea, they began to talk about their philosophies of life. As their discussion went on, they began to argue more and more intensely, each one claiming to know more about life than the other, and they almost came to blows. They realized that neither one would win the argument, so they decided to bring the matter to the local nobleman, who was respected for his wisdom and honesty and who often served as a judge in disputes. The two friends finished their tea in silence and set out to see the nobleman.

When the nobleman had heard the case, he said to the two men, "Whoever answers these three questions correctly will be the one who knows more about life: What is the quickest thing in the world? What is the fattest thing in the world? And what is the sweetest? Return in three days' time with your answers, and I will settle your disagreement."

The tailor returned home and spent the three days thinking about these riddles, but found no answers to them. When the innkeeper returned to his home, he sat down, holding his head in his hands. Just then, his daughter saw him and cried out, "What's wrong, Father?" The innkeeper told her about the three questions. She answered, "Father, when you go back to the nobleman, give him these answers: The quickest thing in the world is thought. The fattest thing is the earth itself. The sweetest is sleep."

When three days had passed, the tailor and the innkeeper came before the nobleman. "Have you found answers to my questions?" he asked. The tailor stood there silently.

But when the innkeeper gave his answers, the nobleman exclaimed, "Wonderful! Those are wonderful answers! But tell me, how did you think of those answers?"

"I must tell you truthfully that those answers were told to me by my daughter," replied the innkeeper.

"Since your daughter knows so much about life," said the nobleman, "I will test her further. Give her this dozen eggs, and see if she can hatch them all in three days. If she does so, she will have a great reward."

The innkeeper carefully took the eggs and returned home. When his daughter saw him carrying a large basket, and she also saw how he trembled, she asked him, "What is wrong, Father?" He showed her the eggs and told her what she must do in order to receive a reward and prove her wisdom again.

The daughter took the eggs, and she weighed them, each one, in her hands. "Dear Father, how can these eggs be hatched when they are cooked? Boiled eggs indeed! But wait, Father, I have a plan as to how to answer this riddle." The daughter boiled some beans and waited three days. Then she instructed her father to go to the nobleman's house and ask permission to plant some special beans.

"Beans?" asked the nobleman. "What sort of special beans?" Taking the beans from his pocket, the innkeeper showed them to the nobleman and said, "These are boiled beans, Your Honor, that I want to plant."

The nobleman burst out laughing and said, "Well, you certainly are not wise to the ways of the world if you don't even know that beans can't grow from boiled beans—only from seeds."

"Well, then," replied the innkeeper, "neither can chickens hatch from boiled eggs!"

The nobleman immediately sensed the clever mind of the innkeeper's daughter in the answer. So he said to the innkeeper, "Tell your daughter to come here in three days. And she must come neither dressed nor undressed, neither walking nor riding, neither hungry nor overfed, and she must bring me a gift that is not a gift."

The innkeeper returned home even more perplexed than before. When his daughter heard what she had to do in three days' time, she laughed and said, "Father, tomorrow I will tell you what to do."

The next day the daughter said to her father, "Go to the marketplace, and buy these things: a large net, some almonds, a goat, and a pair of pigeons." The father was puzzled by these requests, but as he loved his daughter and knew her to be wise, he did not question her. Instead, he went to the marketplace and bought all that she had requested.

On the third day the innkeeper's daughter prepared for her visit to the nobleman. She did not eat her usual morning meal. Instead, she got undressed and wrapped herself in the transparent net, so she was neither dressed nor undressed.

Then she took two almonds in one hand and the pair of pigeons in the other. Leaning on the goat, she held on so that one foot dragged on the ground while she hopped on the other one. In this way, she was neither walking nor riding.

As she approached the nobleman's house, he saw her and came out to greet her.

At the gate she ate the two almonds to show that she was neither hungry nor overfed.

Then the innkeeper's daughter extended her hand, showing the pigeons she intended to give as a gift. The nobleman reached out to take them, but just at that moment the young woman opened her hand to release the pigeons—and they flew away. So she had brought a gift that was not a gift.

The nobleman gave a laugh of approval and called out, "You are a clever woman! I want to marry you, but on one condition. You must promise never to interfere with any of my judgments."

"I will marry you," said the innkeeper's daughter, "but I also have one condition: If I do anything that will cause you to send me away, you must promise to give me whatever I treasure most in your house." They each agreed to the other's condition, and they were married.

Some time passed, and one day a man came to speak with the young wife, who had become known for her wisdom. "Help me, please," the man begged, "for I know you are wise and understand things in ways your husband does not."

"Tell me what is wrong, for you look very troubled, sir," she answered. And the man told her his story.

"Last year," said the man, "my partner and I bought a barn that we now share. He keeps his wagon there, and I keep my horse there. Well, last night my horse gave birth to a foal under the wagon. So my partner says the foal belongs to him. We began to argue and fight, so we brought our dispute to the nobleman. The nobleman judged that my partner was right. I protested but to no avail. What can I do?"

The young woman gave him certain advice and instructions to follow. As she had told him to do, he took a fishing pole, went over to the nobleman's well, and pretended he was fishing there. The nobleman rode by the well, just as his wife had predicted, and when he saw the man, he stopped and asked, "What are you doing?" The man replied, "I am fishing in the well." The nobleman started to laugh and said, "Are you really so stupid that you do not know that you can't catch fish in a well?" "No, sir," said the man, "not any more than I know that a wagon cannot give birth to a foal."

At this answer, the nobleman stopped laughing. Understanding that his wife must be involved in the case, he got out of his carriage and went looking for her. When he found his wife, he said, "You did not keep your promise not to interfere with my judgments, so I must send you back to your father's home."

"You are right, my husband," she said. "But before I leave, let us dine together one last time." The nobleman agreed to this request.

At dinner the nobleman drank a great deal of wine, for his wife kept refilling his cup, and as a result he soon became very sleepy. As soon as he was asleep, the wife signaled to the servants to pick him up and put him in the carriage next to her, and so they returned to her father's home.

The next morning when the nobleman woke up, he looked around and realized where he was. "But how did I get here? What is the meaning of this?" he shouted.

"You may remember, dear husband, that you also made an agreement with me," she answered. "You promised that if you sent me away, I would be able to pick whatever I treasured most in your house to take with me. There is nothing I treasure more than you. So that is how you came to be here with me."

The nobleman laughed, embraced his wife, and said, "Knowing how much you love me, I now realize how much I love you. Let us return to our home."

And they did go home, where they lived with love and respect for many happy years.

Peninnah Schram is an associate professor of speech and drama at Stern College of Yeshiva University. Schram has written several books, including Jewish Stories One Generation Tells Another *and, most recently,* Tales of Elijah the Prophet. *She is the founding director of the Jewish Storytelling Center in New York City, where she lives.*

WILLIE THE BUG-MAN

Susan Klein

Years ago in my kindergarten classroom there was a little blond brown-eyed boy who sparkled when he spoke. Each day he brought a shoe box to school and put it on the long blue shelf that edged the immense south-facing windows in our room. Every box contained a variation on the same theme: bugs. Willie found these fuzzy little six-legged critters—striped, winged, and dotted—in the woods and fields near his house and brought them for us to see.

Willie was more than a collector. He was also a caretaker, for he knew dozens of things about his bugs. He knew where they lived, what they ate, where they went when it rained, and whom they hung out with on Friday nights. He fed them and talked to them and enlightened us with pertinent information concerning them. All this trafficking with bugs earned him the name Willie the Bug-Man.

One day he brought to school a large glass mayonnaise jar, the size restaurants use. His dad and mom had helped him clean it up and hammer a screwdriver point into the cap to make air holes. Inside the jar seven black, white, and greenish-yellow striped caterpillars marched 'round and 'round.

I said, "Willie, those are mighty beautiful caterpillars. Where are we going to put them?"

He said, "On the window shelf with the others."

"Oh, Willie, I don't think that's a good idea. On that shelf the sun beats down so hot that your caterpillars will fry in that glass jar."

"Don't worry about a thing, Miss Klein. Check in here," Willie said as he pointed over his shoulder to his blue backpack.

By this time of the school year, I knew enough to unzip the backpack and peer inside. Willie always had surprises in there. This time I discovered a bouquet of milkweed plants without the pods.

"What's this for, Willie?"

"Shade and food," he said gleefully. Then he took the bouquet,

While giving a workshop many years ago, I began talking about my experience with Willie and his caterpillars as an example of those rare, delicious moments of wonder that teachers sometimes have. Now each time I tell this story, I am reminded of the ways teachers and students can trade roles.

opened the lid, jammed the leafy stems in the jar, and tightened the lid. As he put the jar on the windowsill, we could see the caterpillars already climbing up the stems and hanging upside-down under the leaves. Willie said, "See? Shade."

The next day when we came to school, everyone dashed over to the jar. The leaves were gone, the stems were dry and shriveling, and the caterpillars were once again marching around the bottom of the jar.

"Willie," I said, "what are we going to do for them today?"

"Don't worry about a thing, Miss Klein. Check in here," he said, pointing to his backpack again. There I found another bouquet of milk-weed plants he'd gathered on the way to school. And so it continued. Every day Willie would take out the old stems and install a new serving of shade and food. The caterpillars thrived.

There was another fellow in our room who just loved those caterpillars. Marlon was one of those kids who love to touch things. Every day he would literally wrap himself around the jar and hug it until I could persuade him to try another activity. He simply loved those caterpillars. Some days his "friends," as he called them, would stay on his desk throughout the school day.

During the weeks that followed, we studied caterpillars while ours grew longer and thicker. We saw filmstrips about caterpillars, read stories, drew and painted pictures, wrote poetry, and made caterpillars from egg cartons and pipe cleaners. We even "became" caterpillars.

One day Marlon came up to me and pulled at my skirt with a pathetic look on his face. "Miss Klein," he said, "they're gone."

"Who's gone?"

"My friends!"

I said, "Marlon, come on. How could they be gone? They were much too fat to get through the holes in the lid."

He took my hand and led me to the jar. They *were* gone. I said,

"Marlon, did you let them out?"

"No! Miss Klein, they were my friends. I wouldn't do that. I knew they had to stay in there."

I said, "Well, Marlon, let's wait till Willie the Bug-Man comes. He'll probably know what's happened."

When Willie got to school, Marlon raced to meet him. We all stood around the empty jar. Willie said, "Let's look closer."

I opened the lid, and we all looked in through the top, though we could see perfectly well through the glass jar. In the nick of time I lifted the lid straight up before Marlon could grab the seven cocoons that we could now plainly see hanging from the underside of the lid.

Marlon just looked up, smiling and smiling at the seven lime-green pods that held his friends. Willie said, "Miss Klein, why don't you stick the lid to that high shelf?"

So I did. Using masking tape, I attached the rim of the lid to the underside of my highest library shelf. Each day Marlon would stare at them for a while and then come announce to the class, "Chrysalis report: Light green, gold dots, one black line."

Next day: "Chrysalis report. Still green, with gold dots and one black line."

Next day: "Chrysalis report. Green, no dots, one black line."

Next day: "Chrysalis report. Greenish, no dots, no lines."

Next day: "Chrysalis report. Gray and green."

Finally, one day, he said, "Chrysalis report. Prunes."

We all stopped what we were doing, and everyone said, "*Prunes?*"

"Yeah, prunes," he repeated, with a quizzical look on his face. Marlon was right. The chrysalises were no longer fresh and green—they looked like seven prunes hanging from the lid.

When Marlon asked me what was wrong with them, I couldn't answer very positively. But I did tell him that the situation didn't look good.

The next day we got no chrysalis report: Marlon began crying as soon as he saw them. "Miss Klein, why did my friends have to die?" he said as his little shoulders heaved.

"Marlon, I know you loved them very, very much," I said. "I wish I could tell you why they died. But I can't."

"Can we have a funeral?" he asked in a whisper.

"Well, of course. Tomorrow I'll bring in a special box, and we'll have a ceremony under our maple tree."

He seemed somewhat satisfied with that and spent the rest of the day mourning his friends.

The following day I brought to school an old wooden cigar box painted with palm trees. I envisioned the kids standing in the cemetery across the street from the school, under the maple tree whose changes we observed from our windows all year long. I knew it would be a mighty solemn affair.

But when I got to school, Willie and Marlon were already there, shrieking and jumping up and down outside our classroom windows. When I walked up, they hollered, "Hey, Miss Klein, take a look at this!"

My eyes traveled to the spot the boys were pointing to, and there, on the other side of the glass, I saw seven beautiful monarch butterflies. Willie's eyes were shining, and Marlon was grinning all over himself.

For a bit we just stood there and watched them fluttering. "What do you think of that?" I asked.

"I think you gotta get pretty ugly before you get beautiful again," said Willie.

We went inside, opened all the windows, and propped open the outside door. As the kids came onto the playground, they all ventured by to look at the magic that had taken place. There was much chatter and speculation by the whole school population that day. We kept our coats on once school began and left everything open so that the butterflies could find the breeze and slip away to their new lives to find food and water and a place to rest, as Willie the Bug-Man said they would.

We had a lot of work to do that day, but someone always had an eye on the butterflies' action. When the first one escaped, the watcher's shriek of joy alerted the rest of us, and we laughed and stared in wonder at Marlon's friends flying around. By the end of the day we had heard seven shrieks, and all the butterflies had entered the wider world.

The following school year my class went on to a new teacher. Willie the Bug-Man brought my new class a gift—a large jar of caterpillars. "These new kindergartners need to know how it all really happens," he said. Unfortunately, that batch didn't make it, and the magic of that first year was never repeated.

Shortly thereafter I left my teaching job to go on the road as a touring storyteller. Six years later, in the fall of 1988, as I was preparing to head for Tennessee, I heard a knock at the kitchen door. There stood Willie the Bug-Man, all grown up and in junior high. I hadn't seen him in years.

Silently, he handed me a present wrapped up in fluffy white tissue paper with a big red ribbon. The card read, "It'll always be real special between you and me."

I tugged at the ribbon, and the paper fell away, revealing a large white gauze butterfly with rainbows painted on its wings. Willie and I visited for a bit, while I hung the butterfly in my kitchen.

It still flies there, and when I come home from telling stories all over America, it's the first thing I see as I come in the kitchen door. It still reminds me of the important things that Marlon and Willie the Bug-Man taught me.

Susan Klein of Oak Bluffs, Massachusetts, formerly a public-school teacher and a theater-arts instructor, now tells tales professionally and conducts storytelling workshops. She founded and directs the annual Festival of Storytelling on Martha's Vineyard.

A Fisherman and His Wife

Carol L. Birch

Long ago I read a definition of "the good life" written by Myra Mannes, and it stayed with me. Then in 1985 I taught a storytelling course in a women's prison. One woman told a version of this tale with the three wishes but without the story's traditional enmity. All of this, and more, is here for you.

Once upon a time there was a fisherman named Jacques, who lived with his wife, Monique, in the south of France, where days are warm and nights are balmy. From Jacques they had fresh fish to eat, and from Monique's garden there were fresh vegetables on their table. Fragrant herbs and wildflowers of every hue grew in sweet profusion around their cottage.

But they were not happy. They could not enjoy what they had because they were so bitterly aware of what they did not have. Try as they might, they could not get ahead, so they greeted each day with fear and anxiety. Fear narrowed their vision, and anxiety left them with a bitter taste in their mouths.

One day Jacques caught a magic fish who promised three wishes over a year and a day, and they believed that they would finally know true contentment in their lives. Monique and Jacques talked late into the night, and the next morning at dawn Jacques went down to the sea and called out as he had been instructed:

> *Fishy, fishy in the sea,*
> *Prithee cometh unto me.*
> *Monique and her husband, Jacques,*
> *Have a wish for you to grant.*

The fish leaped above the dazzling sea and asked, "What do you wish?" "My wife and I wish to be prosperous vineyard owners!" replied Jacques. "Go in peace," called out the fish. "It is just as you wish."

Jacques ran down the road, past the small cottage that had once been home, eagerly searching for Monique. He saw her in the distance, pacing, wearing a nervous smile and a lovely gown. Together they gave the laborers in the fields and the servants in their new mansion the day off so that the two could revel privately in their new-found luxuries.

The next day Jacques began the life of a prosperous vineyard owner. He had known such cold from his days at sea that he looked forward to working on warm and dry land. And at first he was happy. He said the chill was finally gone from his bones. But soon the dust of the earth filled his eyes and mouth. The sun seemed to beat relentlessly upon his back. Eventually, he became more miserable than he had ever been as a fisherman.

Now, Monique was also happy with her new life—at first. But she had never managed servants before, and she was uncertain in her role. Worst of all, the women in town would not receive her, while the wives of the fishermen were suspicious of her new wealth and ways.

After six months of this life the dissatisfied couple decided to use their second wish, and Jacques once again called on the magic fish at the break of day:

> *Fishy, fishy in the sea,*
> *Prithee cometh unto me.*
> *Monique and her husband, Jacques,*
> *Have a wish for you to grant.*

"Are you happy?" asked the fish. "No, my wife and I wish that I would be the mayor of the village." "Go in peace," said the fish. "Your wish is granted."

Jacques passed their small cottage and looked at it longingly. As he passed the vineyard, he spat on the ground. About a mile from town he saw a crowd of people waiting . . . for him? One wanted to know what he intended to do about a land dispute, another demanded an appointment in private, and a third shrieked at him for failing to find more water for the town.

Jacques and Monique had dreams of what their lives would now be like. Which dreams came true? Oh, they seemed to be treated less suspiciously, but behind their backs the gossiping went on relentlessly. Now the women in town had to receive Monique, but they did not accept her. As for Jacques, he was free from the chill of the sea and the dust of the land, but his office brought unforeseen demands. He wanted to be a good mayor, so he spent hours hearing disputes and still longer hours considering them. When he wasn't at work, he was thinking of work. It seemed that someone was always unhappy. And most often it was his wife.

Feeling more and more isolated, Monique began visiting the small cottage where she and Jacques had lived. She transplanted wildflowers and herbs from the hills to their yard. She twined wild roses about the door. She enjoyed the labors that she had abhorred—hoeing the garden, whitewashing the cottage, weaving covers and curtains and carpets. If she just sat in the mayor's residence, the hours dragged on. At the cottage, while she worked, the time flew. But her thoughts always went back to the final wish that dangled enticingly before her. She wondered what would release them from their fear and anxiety, which had only deepened.

After just three months Monique suggested a final wish. "Go to the fish, and ask to be the King of France! You'll have councilors for all the tiresome duties, and we'll have parties. When you have to work, I will have the theater, the opera, and ballets to attend. No one will dare to talk against us!"

Because Jacques did not oppose her, Monique thought he agreed with her. The next day Jacques called out a final time:

> *Fishy, fishy in the sea,*
> *Prithee cometh unto me.*
> *Monique and her husband, Jacques,*
> *Have a wish for you to grant.*

"Are you happy?" asked the fish. "No," said Jacques sorrowfully, "this is not the life for us." "What do you seek?" the fish called out above the swelling sea. "Well, my wife wants me to be the King of France, but I do not think I am any better suited to that life." "What do you wish?" the fish inquired. "Oh, my wish is not so simple. I want my wife and me to find contentment, and I do not know where it is." "Go in peace," said the fish. "Your wish has come true." Then the fish disappeared, never to be seen again.

Jacques walked slowly back toward town. When he came to the small cottage where he and Monique had lived, he saw her there with her back bent over the garden. Once again she wore an old and shabby dress. But when Monique looked up, her smile was radiant. She ran to Jacques, and they kissed and kissed again. "Oh, Husband, you wished well! I had forgotten all that we had."

So Jacques and Monique began to live their old lives anew. They enjoyed living in the south of France, where the days are warm and the nights are balmy. They savored the fresh fish and vegetables on their table. They reveled in the fragrant herbs and wildflowers of every hue that grew in sweet profusion around their cottage. And, oh, they lived contentedly and much more happily ever after.

Carol L. Birch of Southbury, Connecticut, is noted for the integrity of her renderings of literary stories and folk tales. An adjunct teacher of storytelling for Wesleyan University and a librarian, Birch is also an award-winning recording artist and producer.

THE TWO SONS

Alice McGill

I first heard about the bogyman when I was a little girl. My father used him often to make me and my sisters and brothers behave. "If you don' get in that bed and go to sleep, that bogyman's gon' get you." I never could imagine what he looked like, and that faceless bogyman lay hidden in my imagination until I called him up for "The Two Sons."

Once in a little community near Dismal Swamp, there lived a pretty young woman who had two little boys to raise by herself. Her husband had sickened and died during the Big War. He had fought bravely and in many battles too. But somehow or another a terrible sickness came over him, and he was sent home from over the seas to die.

Just before death claimed him, he called his sons to his bedside. His dear wife held his hand as he instructed each son in kind: "Mind your manners, work hard, pay respect to all old folks, don't ever sass your mama, stay away from the swamp, and no matter what happens to me . . . if you listen to what I have told you, you will never have to worry about—"

The poor man died before he could utter his last words. Oh, what a pitiful sight he made. The grieving widow did the best she could to comfort her two sons.

After the burial, friends and neighbors brought comfort to the small family by way of fine food and lively talk. Just at sunset the friends and neighbors departed to their homes through the woods and around the swamp. Then the two sons helped their mother. One lit the oil lamp, and the other kindled a fire in the wood stove to chase off the cool of the evening. Their mother seemed to be at peace, and she was smiling as the three of them chatted around the fire. At last, one of them ventured to ask his mother if she knew what their father's last words might have been if he had been able to say them before he passed on.

The woman paced the floor as she answered, "Oh, my sons, just do as your father said. Mind your manners, work hard, pay respect to all old folks, don't ever sass your mama, stay away from the swamp, and you will never have to worry." But worry and grief beat at her chest. She did not tell them that their father's meager pension would not pay for the cost of keeping the house, let alone put food on the table and clothes on their backs. Before long she found a job weaving large reed baskets for a storekeeper.

The sons thought about their father's last words many nights after their mother had fallen into exhausted sleep. Over and over they repeated the last sentence to each other. They filled in the missing words from their deepest thoughts.

"You will never have to worry about paying bills." "You will never have to worry about finding a job, making a fortune, ruling the world . . . " They could not think of suitable words. Some years passed, and as the sons grew taller and stronger, the memory of their father grew dimmer and dimmer. Finally, they could not remember his face at all, and his last words to them left their restless minds. Their mother, however, worked hard to keep food on the table. Time after time she reminded her sons to feed the chickens, water the garden, and keep the yard clean. Dutifully the sons obeyed, for a while.

One summer day while they were sprinkling the garden, an old man appeared at the garden gate.

"How 'bout givin' me two of them cucumbers?" he begged. "I'm so hungry I can eat 'em right off the vine."

The sons screamed, one after the other, "Why don't you plant your own garden?" One son sprinkled the old man so that he hobbled off dripping wet. The other son threw his watering can. The can bounced off the old man's back. As he whimpered away in pain, the sons laughed.

Just before sundown their mother returned from her basket weaving. Thinking she would be pleased, the sons eagerly told her what they had done to protect the family garden. She was not pleased.

"Shame on you for treatin' a poor old man so. We have a gracious plenty in our garden. Why didn't you give him two cucumbers?"

"He didn't have no rights on our cucumbers!" one of the sons screamed at his mother. "If you think I'm goin' to give away good food to any ol' beggar, you must be silly. I'm tired of waterin' this old garden anyhow."

The other son bragged, "Glad I hit him with my can. I'll hit him again if I want to, and you can't stop me."

Their mother was so shocked over the change in her sons that she could barely speak. "Go in the house," she muttered. "I will talk to you in a little while." She turned and walked toward the chinaberry tree.

The two sons stormed through the front door, thinking that she was going to switch them. Then they eased through the back door and ran to the swamp to hide among the marsh reeds.

The muddy green water sloshed against their knees as they stumbled about, trying to find solid ground. When at last they thought they were safe, their feet began to sink into quicksand.

The more they struggled, the deeper they sank, until a rope was thrown around the upper part of their bodies. They felt themselves being pulled out of the mire and along the rough ground. The holder of the other end of the rope was hidden in darkness, but they heard a deep gruff voice grow louder and louder as the tug of the rope pulled them nearer and nearer.

The voice was saying, "Mind your manners, work hard, pay respect to all old folks, don't ever sass your mama, stay away from the swamp, and you will never have to worry about . . . the BOGYMAN!" The two sons were never heard of or seen again.

Alice McGill of Columbia, Maryland, taught school for 20 years before embarking on a storytelling and film career in 1976. She specializes in African-American folk tales and is widely known for her portrayal of Sojourner Truth, the former slave who became a crusader for civil rights.

JACK AND THE SILVER KEYS

Duncan Williamson

It was in a wee rundown farm in the country that Jack stayed with his mother. It had been a good farm at one time, but it went to wreck and ruin through the neglect of Jack's father. Jack was reared up by his mother, and he and she ran the wee bit [small] farm between them. But they ran it mostly down to the ground, and things went from bad to worse. They had an old horse and an old cow and a couple of pigs, but they were forced to sell them, and things got very bad indeed.

Jack said to his mother one day, "If things dinna pick up a bit, I doubt [suppose] I'll have to go and look for a job."

"Son," she said, "it's no a job you're needin'; you need to do some work about the place. It wouldna be in this state if you'd spend more time on it. It's a farm, and if you would work harder and plow some of the ground and dae some work about it, you could make it pay."

So Jack made up his mind that he was going to do a little work on the farm. Looking at a field beside his house that had never been plowed for years, he told his mother, "Mother, probably the best thing I can dae is get a lane [loan] o' a pair o' horses and a plow, and plow that field and sow a puckle [small amount] of corn or something into it."

So he got up in the morning, had his wee bit o' breakfast, and went to the neighboring farm, where he asked for a lane o' a pair o' horses and a plow.

The man was amazed when Jack asked him, and he said, "What are you going to do with it?"

"Well," Jack said, "It came to ma mind that me and my mother canna survive much longer if we dinna get something done. Our wee bit o' place is gettin' run doon."

And the farmer said, "That's a good farm. I'll lend you a pair o' horses and a plow if you want to plow that bit ground. Mind, Jack, there are a lot o' stanes [stones] into it; it hasna been plowed since your father plowed it years before. In fact, it was wonst a moor."

Since 1976 I've been recording the hundreds of traditional stories I know for the School of Scottish Studies at Edinburgh University. This story was passed down to me from my father's family, a clan of nomadic tinsmiths and basket-makers who relied on stories for their education and survival. I tell the stories of my tradition so that the old traveling folk will never be forgotten.

175

"It'll no matter," Jack said, "I'll be as careful as I can with your plow." So Jack got a lane o' the plow and a pair o' horses from the farmer and took them home. The next morning after breakfast time he went out and started. He was plowing up and down, plowing up and down, plowing up and down, and the gulls were following behind him, picking the worms up. And he turned some turf with his plow. He wasn't pleased because this part of the furrow wasn't laid down. When he went back and tried to push it down with his foot, he looked in the furrow and saw something sticking up.

He said, "God bless us, what's that?" And he bent down and picked up three large keys on a ring. Jack said to himself, "In the name o' God, hoo did that get there—three large keys?" Every key was nearly a foot long. Jack looked at them, "God bless us," he said, "they're no made o' iron; iron doesna get that color, and they're no rusty." He hung them on the shaft of the plow and plowed away till about evening.

Then he came in and had his wee bit supper, and he cracked [talked] to his mother. "Oh, Mother, I've a funny thing," he said, "tae tell ye: when I was plowing today that field you tellt me was never plowed for years, I picked up the queerest thing you ever seen."

She said, "What was it, Jack?"

He said, "Mother, three big keys onto a ring!"

"No!" she said.

He said, "Aye, Mother, three big keys."

"Jack, Jack," she said, "you dinna ken what you've found!"

"Ha, Mother," he said, "I ken what I found—I found three keys!"

"Aye," she said, "Jack, you found three keys, but you were only a laddie when these keys wis lost. You dinna ken the story behind these keys. These keys is made o' silver. Sit doon there, and I'll tell ye. These keys were the cause o' your father's death and the cause o' this farm gettin' run-doon till there's nothing hardly left, it's no worth nothing!

Many, many years ago—15, to be exact—when you were a bit o' a bairn here, this was a thrivin' farm. Your father was a good man and a good worker, and we had everything we wanted.

"But the king came to visit in the country. In those times there used to be a lot of wild boars and a lot of hunting about here. On his rounds, when he stayed near here with the lord o' the district, they went for a boar hunt. And across that wee field belongin' to your father the king lost those three silver keys. And the king was never kent to be without these keys: wherever he went, these keys hung to his belt. And they went a-missin'.

"Everybody searched high and low. He promised the body that would find the three keys that he'd give them the greatest reward that ever they could ask for. There were hundreds and thousands that searched for them keys, and they could never get them. The king stayed here for nearly a month, searching—there were thousands o' folk huntin' for them keys!

"It drove your father beyond endurance. He gave up his work, let the farm run in ruin, and spent the entire days o' his life searching—because the king said he'd make any man the richest in the country if he could get him them keys. What they meant to the king nobody knows, but his entire life depended on them. Your father searched night and day, and he never done a hand's turn but was oot every day searchin' for these keys. And one night in a night of fog he went a-missin'. He never came hame, and they found his body lyin' drowned in a ditch. That's what happened to your father. Now, Jack, you've got the king's keys. It's exactly 15 years since these keys were lost. What are you going to do with them?"

"Well, Mother," he said, "what can I dae with them?"

"Well," she said, "I hope they bring ye better luck as they brought yir father. The best thing you could do with them, Jack, is tak them back to the king. Tak them in, polish them, clean them up. They'll no be hard to clean. And tak them back. I suppose the king'll be an older man now, but I think he's still the same king. It's a long distance from here, mind ye, tae where the king stays in the capital city, but anybody'll tell ye the road, and ye canna go wrong. I'm telling ye for yir ain guid: keep them hidden, and dinna tell naebody ye have them but the king."

"Well, Mother," he said, "they're no my property, and if a king . . . Well, I'm no worried about the reward."

"Oh, Jack," she said, "ye'll be highly rewarded if ye can get tae the king wi them. But if ye ever breathe a word aboot the keys, ye'll never see the king alive because ye'll be robbed and murdered, and they'll be tooken from ye. Forget about everything here, Jack. Never mind, I'll get the laddie from the neighboring farm tae finish that wee bit plowing and sow a wee puckle corn to keep us goin'. But the best thing you can do is tomorrow mornin' pack up yir wee bit o' gear, tak a wee bite wi ye, and get them keys back to the king. I suppose you'll get the reward, and I'm tellin' ye, it'll be nae wee reward at that! But will ye dae me one favor?"

"Well, Mother," he said, "you're my mother—what would ye want me tae dae?"

"That was the cause o' yir father's ruin," she said, "and I would like to ken what they're fir and what they open."

"Well, Mother," he said, "I'll try my best tae find oot for ye."

"Okay then," she said, "that's a promise."

So the next morning, true to his word, Jack got up early, had his wee bit breakfast, made a wee parcel o' meat to himself—whatever he had about the house—put the best bits o' clothes he had on him, and said goodbye to his mother. He set sail [started traveling] on the road. And he walked and walked and walked. He asked folk this, and he asked folk that, but he kept the keys hidden in the lining of his jacket. He wouldn't show them to a soul.

But he must have been on the road for three or four weeks, and his clothes began to get tattered and torn. He got kind o' rough—he never shaved and barely took time to wash his face, and his boots began to get worn down. Finally, he made his way to the capital city, where the king's palace was. Now, he didn't go straight away to the palace, demanding an interview with the king. He wandered about the town two or three times, asking this and asking that, finding all he could find out. But finally he found out that the king was home and his queen was home, and Jack made his way to the king's palace. The first body he met at the palace was a guard.

And the guard stopped him, saying, "Where do you think you're goin'? Where do you think *you're* goin' tae?"

"Well," said Jack, "I want to see the king."

The guard looked at him. "You," he said, "want to see the king? What do you want to see the king for?"

"I've got a wee message for him," Jack said. "I want to speak tae him."

He said, "You tell me, and I'll tell the king."

"No," said Jack, "I'm no tellin' you what I've got to tell the king." And a heated argument arose between them.

But just by good luck, who came walking up behind the guard's back but the king himself, an aged man, about 60 years old. "What's goin' on here," he said, "guard?"

"Your Majesty," he said, "it's this rough-lookin' character of a man here who wants an interview wi you, the king."

"Well," said the king, and he looked at Jack, "he seems a fine specimen o' a man tae me. He's probably a traveler on the road. He's one of my subjects, I suppose." The king said, "Where do you come from, young man?"

"To tell you the truth," Jack said, "Your Majesty," and he bowed to the king, "I came a long way to get here." Jack told him he came from such-and-such a place, and he said, "I came tae see ye. In fact, I brought a present for ye."

"Well," said the king, and he smiled, "you brought a present for me. This is very good o' you! Come with me."

The guard wasn't very well pleased. As Jack walked past him, the guard looked daggers at Jack—you know, Jack with his rough coat.

The king walked into his chamber with Jack and told Jack to sit down. The king sat down too. "Well, my young man," he said, "would you care for a drink?"

"To tell you the truth," Jack said, "Your Majesty, drink is a thing I could never afford. I've never had very much time for it."

"Anyway," he said, "you'll have a glass of wine with me before you tell me your story." The king was very pleasant, and he called for two beautiful glasses of wine, and he and Jack drank the wine together. "Now," he said, "young man, what have you got for me? What have you come to see me about?"

Jack rammed his hand down into his coat, under his arm. From a big long pocket he pulled out the three keys, and he held them in front of the king.

As the king looked, his eyes came out in his head. And the king started to shake—the excitement got the better o' him. For a minute he couldn't speak. "Young man," he said, "do ye know what you've got there?"

"To tell you the truth, Your Majesty," he said, "tae me they're three keys."

He said, "Where did you get these keys?"

"Well," he said, "you, when I was only an infant, were huntin' a boar across my father's land, a wee farm."

"I remember it well," said the king.

Jack said, "You came for a visit to your country to see some o' your landowners. I believe ye lost these keys." And he told the king his name was Jack.

"Well, Jack, you don't know what you've done for me."

Jack said, "I never done nothing for you, Your Majesty; they're your property, and my mother advised me . . . "

"By the way, how is your mother?" the king said. "I remember a long time ago stopping by her little farm to water the horses, and she was a pleasant woman."

Jack said, "My father died searching for your keys."

"Oh, bad luck," said the king, "very bad."

"He searched," he said, "his entire life for to get your keys. One night in a fog and mist he was lost. He ended up drowned in a ditch."

"Oh, I'm very sad," said the king, "very sad to hear about that. And you, my young man, how did you come by these keys?"

Jack said, "Me and my mother had a wee bit argument aboot the farm gettin' run doon, but I didna ken nothin' aboot the keys; she never tellt me. Prob'ly if she had tellt me about the keys, I would hae ended up the same as my father, searchin' fir them."

"Ha!" the king said with a smile, "you'll prob'ly be after the reward too."

"Well," said Jack, "it would come in handy."

"Oh, but," he said, "don't worry, my young man, you'll be highly rewarded."

"But, Your Majesty," Jack said, "will ye do one thing for me? Will you tell me what these keys is fir?"

"Well, Jack, I'll tell ye," he said. "I'll tell ye part o' the story, but I can only tell ye the first half; I canna tell ye the second. I had a great friend here belonging tae me many, many years ago who lived in the court wi me. He was a wise old man—a court magician. And him and I used tae be the greatest o' friends. But he had to go away back tae his own land, he never mentioned where, and before he left, he gave me three silver keys. These three keys opens three gates tae a special garden. I used tae go and visit that garden whenever I felt the mood takin' me. But then I lost the keys, and thereafter I could never enter through the gates of that garden."

"Well, Your Majesty," Jack said, "I'm very happy you can go back to your garden."

"Jack," he said, "you've no idea what you've done for me. Ye've made me a new man! I want you," he said, "to be highly rewarded! You can have the whole privilege o' the palace. You can have everything you want. But you must make me a promise that you shall not leave for 20 days, till I come back. I'm goin' on a visit. But I want you to have everything that you require under the sun. Don't spare anything!"

Then the king called for the head cook, and he called for the head footman. He called for the head o' the guards, and he warned them all, and called for the queen, tellt them, "Jack must have the run o' the palace—see that he wants for nothing. But," he said to Jack, "have another drink." So he and Jack sat and had another drink. They cracked away about good things—he was a very pleasant man, the king.

"Now, Jack," he said, "a footman'll show ye to your room. And I want you to stay there. Make me a promise that you'll not leave the palace or the district for 20 days till I come home." So the king bade goodbye to Jack and said, "I'll no be seein' ye in the morning, but remember, I'll see ye as soon as I come back."

So Jack went down to the dining hall, and he had a good time to himself. He had plenty to eat and plenty to drink; he had a nice clean-up, a right bath, and a nice change o' clothes. He really enjoyed himself. Then the footman showed him to a lovely bed, and he lay down on it and relaxed. But he hadn't been in bed for more than an hour when he heard a knock on the door.

Jack got up. "Who's there?" he said.

"Oh, it's me, the queen. I want to talk to you," she said very sternly.

Jack opened the door, came out, and bowed to Her Majesty. "Your

Majesty, what can I do for you?"

"It's no what you can do for me," she said, "it's what I'm going to do for you."

"Your Majesty," he said, "I have everything I need."

"Oh, you've everything you need, have you? Well, you're gaunna get more than you need," she said, and she came in and shut the door behind her. She said, "You know what you've done?"

"Well," Jack said, "I've done nothing. I've nothing to be ashamed of . . . " Jack thought maybe he had talked rough to some o' the lassies when he had a wee drink with some o' the maids in the palace or something. He tried to think back to what he had done, but he couldn't think on what he could have done to annoy the queen. He racked his brains and said to himself, "I must hae done something to annoy the queen."

The queen was standing there, terrible wicked and wild. There was no reasoning with her.

Jack went down on his knees. "Your Majesty," he said to the queen, "what have I done that makes you so upset?"

"You!" she said. "I was happy and happily married tae the king . . . but you have come and destroyed my life!"

"Oh," Jack said, "Your Majesty, I never destroyed your life. I never done any harm. All I done is come here and give the king back his keys."

"That's what you've done," she said. "Destroyed my life by givin' the king back his keys."

"Well," he said, "I didna know about this." But there was no reasoning with the queen, and the more she talked, the angrier she got. So Jack begged her to tell him the truth about the keys.

"One night," she said, "when the king was drunk, he told me the story." Jack began to cock up his lugs [listen]—he wanted to find out.

She said, "His good friend the wizard, before he left, built a secret garden in the middle of the mountains and guarded it by three gates, so that nothing in the world could ever enter unless the gates were to be opened by the three silver keys. And in that garden is a fountain, the Fountain o' Youth. Whoever spends a day there in that fountain loses a year o' his life; for every day that he spends, he gets younger by a year. So now," she said, "I was happy with the king, growing old with the king. What's gaunna happen to me now, when the king comes back a young man and me an old woman? What will he do? He'll cast me aside like a bit o' stick and take some young woman for his queen. *You* are the cause o' that!" And she got angrier and angrier. She called to the guards, "Arrest that man! He insulted me."

Immediately the guards came and arrested Jack, throwing him in the dungeon. He was taken before the court the next morning, and the penalty for insulting the queen was death. Jack was to be hanged by the neck until he was dead for insulting the queen! There was no escape for him. There he lay in a wee puckle straw, the rats running over the top o' him days out and days in, fed on as little as possible and given barely a drink o' water. Jack said to himself, "I wish to God I had never seen the silver keys."

Anyway, the days passed by, and Jack lost count of time. He barely knew day from night from a wee bit light shining through a slit in the wall in the dungeon. His beard grew long, and his coat got tattered, and the worse he got. Then one day the door was flung open, and in marched three guards, who pulled Jack to his feet and said, "Come on, get on your feet, you insulter of the royalty. Today you're gaunna be hung."

So Jack was marched out to the square, where the scaffold was built, and hundreds of people were all around, waiting to see him hung. They were shouting and flinging stones at him as he was pulled by the guards. The guards were trying at the same time to hold the people back—to think that somebody, a stranger, would come into their district and insult Her Majesty the Queen! It was a great disgrace; it could never be lived down. The guards stood Jack up, made him march up the 13 steps to the scaffold, and put the rope 'round his neck.

The hangman said, "Your last request before you get hung?"

Jack said, "I've no request to make. But if this is the way that ye treat a poor innocent man," he said, "who came into your country with a present and a good greeting for the king . . . and I never insulted the queen!" He pleaded and probbed with [begged] the man, but it was no use.

The hangman was just ready to pull the trap to let Jack hang, when down through the crowd o' folk came a horseman. And a voice rang out, "The king, the king! Make way for the king!" The man rode up, right beside the scaffold, jumped off his horse, ran up the 13 steps, took his sword, cut the rope from around Jack's neck, and led him back down the steps.

"Thank God," Jack said, "somebody's saved me!"

"Jack, Jack," the man said, "what happened to ye?"

Jack looked. The voice was familiar, but Jack didn't know who the man was.

He said, "Jack, do you no ken me?"

"No," said Jack, "I dinna ken you."

All the people went down on their knees. "Back, go back," he said to them, "make way for the king!" He said, "Jack, come with me, I want to speak to ye."

Jack was glad to be saved, and he said to himself, "I'm no carin' who he is. He definitely saved my life—he's a king to me!" Jack was mesmerized as the man lifted him and rode him up through the crowd o' folk. The folk left an opening and let them pass by. The man took him right up to the king's palace. In they went to the great chambers.

The man called for two glasses o' wine and handed one to Jack, who was so shaken with fright that he could hardly drink it. "Calm yourself,

Jack," he said, "you're safe now. Nothing's gaunna bother ye; ye're home and I'm home."

Jack was still amazed. This young man in his forties—Jack didn't know who he was. The man said, "Jack, do you still no ken me? I'm your king."

"Ha!" said Jack. "Well you're no the same king that left here afore I went into that dungeon."

"Aye," he said, "Jack, I'm the same king."

"Oh, aye!" said Jack, "Well, will ye do me one thing, will ye tell me aboot it? I'm lost, and I'm in a terrible state—I was near hung! I was charged . . . "

"I know what you're charged with," said the king. "That's why I rescued you. But don't fear, don't fret; everything's gaunna be all right. Sit down and calm yirsel, take a good glass o' wine, and we'll talk it over. You tell me your story first, Jack, the truth. And I'll tell you mine."

"Well," Jack said, "after I bade goodnight to ye, I enjoyed myself, and I went to the ballroom. I had a few drinks, and I had a good feast. I had a good wash, and I went to bed, and then the queen came in. She accused me of comin' here wi a present for you, the keys. She tellt me that you would ride tae the Garden o' Youth, stay there for 20 days, and come back 20 year younger, and then you would have no more time for her. I tried tae reason wi her, but it was no use. And she said I had insulted her and called the guards, so I was arrested and thrown in the dungeon. And I must hae lay in the dungeon for 20 days."

"Oh," the king said, "you look in a terrible state, but never mind, Jack! For the 20 days you spent in the dungeon, she'll spend the same!" He said to the guards, "Send for the queen immediately."

The queen was sent for, and when she came in, he told the queen, "Sit down there. You know what you've done? Now own up! What did Jack dae tae ye? Now, don't tell me any lies. I want the truth!"

"I knew," she said, "that Jack brought back the keys to you, and you would go . . . " and she started to greet [weep]. "You would go to the Garden o' Youth, and you would come back a young man. You would have no more time for me—you would prob'ly take a young queen, and I'd be cast aside. I accused him; he was the cause o' it."

And he said, "You, for that, would get a young man hung in my absence? Woman, you ought to be ashamed o' yirsel. You, my queen that spent your entire life with me, think that I would do a thing like that on you! My full intention, after I had had my spell in the Garden o' Youth, was to send *you* to the Garden o' Youth for your spell. You're still my queen, and you're still my wife. I love you. But if you think that anybody else could take your place with me, then you're not *fit* to be my queen! I'm not gaunna forgive ye; you are going to the dungeon for the same length o' time that Jack spent in the dungeon: for 20 days! And by that time you'd better think over it . . . you're gaunna suffer the way that poor Jack suffered, the man that gave me eternal life!" He said to the guards, "Take her away!"

Away went the guards with the queen, who was put in the dungeon.

Then the king ordered for Jack to get everything he required under the sun, and he and Jack sat down and had a good drink. He said, "Jack, I must apologize for the queen."

And Jack said, "Well, I was nearly hung, and it's an awfa thing to be nearly hung."

"Oh," said the king, "it's a bad thing to experience, I believe it! But let her suffer—she'll be all right."

"No," said Jack, "no. My poor old mother is back hame, and she'll be worried about me. I couldna go back to my mother and tell her that the queen spent 20 days in a dungeon. I'm a man, and I could tak it. But no, our queen couldna spend 20 days in a dungeon."

The king said, "Jack, is that the truth? Are you ready to forgive the queen for nearly gettin' you your death?"

Jack said, "Aye."

The king rose and clapped Jack on the back. "Jack," he said, "you're a better man than me. But I'll tell ye something," he said, "she's going to apologize to you when she comes back."

So the king sent for the queen, and the guards brought her out in front of the king and Jack.

The king turned to the queen, and he smiled and laughed and said, "You, my queen, sent this young man nearly to his death, and now *he's* gaunna pardon *you*. I was going to put you in the dungeon for 20 days, but he wouldna allow it. He is the greatest friend that ever I have had. And tomorrow I'm takin' ye for a journey to the Garden o' Youth."

The queen was so excited that both the king and Jack had forgiven her that she started to cry again, and she called for one o' her maids. Jack turned 'round to the king and said, "Your Majesty, I think it's time that I was going to see my old mother."

"Well," said the king, "we'll be goin' in the mornin' anyway. But remember, Jack, you're no goin' withoot your reward!"

The queen said to one o' her maids, "Go into my bed chamber and bring me one o' the finest diamond necklaces that I possess. And give it to Jack to take back to his mother in token of my gratitude for saving me from 20 days in the dungeon."

Then the king went ben [to a room further in] and came out with two bags of gold. He placed them on the table and said to Jack, "Jack, that's for you; that's your reward. Now go to my stables and get the finest horse you can find. And the finest suit o' clothes and anything else you want under the sun—just take it for the asking." Then the queen and king bade Jack goodbye, and the king said, "Remember, Jack, if you ever come my way, don't be feared to stop in, because you're my greatest friend."

Jack said, "If you keep carrying on and gettin' younger the way ye dae, I'll prob'ly no recognize ye."

"You'll recognize me, Jack," he said, "because if you dinna visit me, I'll come and visit you. And you never ken—maybe someday *you* might take a wee trip to the Garden o' Youth."

The next morning Jack packed up, took his two bags o' gold and his diamond necklace, got a fine horse, and rode back to his mother. And when he sat down, he told his mother the same story as I'm telling you. He bought a great big farm with all his gold, and he became a big farmer. And he may still be around to this day, because I heard late in the story that Jack and the king paid a visit to the Garden o' Youth. And that's the last o' my story.

Duncan Williamson of Fife, Scotland, was born in a tinker's tent on the shores of Loch Fyne in 1928. He grew up in a family of traveling singers, pipers, and raconteurs and has been called "the national monument of British storytelling." Williamson continues to collect, publish, and perform the stories of his homeland.

C-R-A-Z-Y

Donald Davis

I first heard stories from my Grandmother Walker when I was growing up in Haywood County, North Carolina. But it was from my Uncle Frank, a man who could turn any event into a story, that I learned the power and excitement of story creation. Here is a tale I tell about one of the characters I have known—someone who was crazy in a most positive way.

Mother had worked her way through teacher's college and then taught school for four years before she and Daddy ran away and got married. I was born the next year, and Joe-brother followed a year later. As soon as we were both old enough to be in school, Mother did what she had been waiting for since marriage: she went back to teaching.

Joe-brother and I both went to Sulphur Springs School, less than a mile from our house, but the only job Mother could get was teaching second grade at East Street School, more than three miles away and on the east side of town.

This created what Daddy described as a "transportation dilemma." Mother was one of those people who had to be both first and last on the scene. She considered herself a failure if she did not get to school in the morning before the janitor arrived. Neither would she think of leaving until after the principal had gone home in the afternoon.

The transportation dilemma was that Mother took us to Sulphur Springs School on her way to East Street in the morning, then picked us up on her way home in the afternoon. Her determination to be first and last resulted in our being deposited on the school steps in the morning long before our building was unlocked and in our being locked out in the afternoon while we waited for her.

Joe-brother and I didn't consider this a problem in warm weather; we simply played in the schoolyard early and late. But with the coming of October frost and shorter days, our locked-out times at school grew increasingly uncomfortable.

"Why can't we walk home?" we asked again and again. "We can almost see our house."

"It's not safe for children to go home to an empty house." That was the answer. No more questions were to be asked.

Joe-brother asked anyway. "Why is it safe to freeze to death on the school steps but it's not safe to go home where it's warm?" There seemed to be no answer.

The question must have taken hold, however, for in less than a week Mother gave us a new set of after-school instructions. "As soon as the bell rings this afternoon"—she was using her you-better-listen voice and pointing straight at both of us—"you are to walk, together, on the left side of the road, as straight as you can go, to Miss Annie Macintosh's house. She will take care of you until I get home and pick you up."

Miss Annie became our after-school babysitter. Her house was only a few hundred yards from ours, up Richland Road on the side of a small hill that jutted from the base of Plott's Knob Mountain. It was a wonderful house. Painted white, almost Victorian, the two-story house had five sides, including the big bay windows in front. It had porches above and below, and the roof, covered with fancy scalloped tin shingles, ran up its five wedge-shaped slopes to a point at the very top. The point was topped by a lightning rod with a blue glass ball in the middle and a fluted cable that ran from it to a metal stake driven in the ground near the porch. On the fifth side a one-story kitchen stuck out, stopping the porches from going all the way around and breaking the symmetry of the whole.

If the outside was wonderful, with its soft, grassy lawns and the shade of huge hemlock trees, the inside was just as much fun for 6- and 7-year-olds. There were two sets of stairs. The first was a wide set that curved up the wall near the front door and had a banister you could slide down, if you were careful to stop before hitting the post at the bottom. The back stairs were narrow and secret, with doors at the top and bottom, running from the back of the upstairs hall to the kitchen below.

Joe-brother and I loved to go to Miss Annie's house, not only after school but on Saturdays and Sundays as well. When school was out, we went almost every day throughout the summertime.

The big house had three inhabitants. First there was Miss Annie. She was *old*. She may have been 50, or she may have been 90. When you are

7 years old, there is little difference. She was probably in her eighties.

She was widowed very early in her life by what she called "the way old McKinley messed up Grover Cleveland's little play war," an allusion to her husband's death in Cuba in the Spanish-American War. This early widowhood—so long ago that the honorary title "Miss" had been returned to her—had left her alone with three sons and one daughter to raise.

Miss Annie's father, old Colonel Steward, had been, in her words, "killed by a bunch of Kirk's scoundrels over about Unicoi, Tennessee, in the Northern Aggression." He had come home, before she was old enough to remember him, in a pine box covered with a Confederate battle flag. She kept the flag, folded, at the bottom of her chest of drawers.

Though the circumstances of her life had made her what Daddy called "a patron saint of lost causes," her severe Calvinism allowed her no pity. In spite of what seemed to us to be plenty of contrary evidence, she would severely proclaim that "People get what they deserve." We heard the words again and again. Every emotion, every possible event in human life, from birth to death, from success to failure, fell under the leveling gavel of that one phrase: "People get what they deserve."

The second occupant of the Macintosh house was Miss Annie's only daughter, Mary Catherine. Mary Catherine seemed to Joe-brother and me to be about 7 years old, for she liked to play all the same things we played. In truth she was nearly 50, a perpetual 7-year-old adult who Daddy said "couldn't quite take care of herself."

If she had been born in a different time or place, she surely would have been tested and specially schooled. But in the generation in which she was born, and in Sulphur Springs, the choice was conventional public school or no school at all.

Miss Annie had, in fact, enrolled her at Sulphur Springs School at age 6, more than 40 years before we knew her. Every day for the first week Mary Catherine had been walked to school and then home again by Miss

Annie. On Friday of the first week, when Miss Annie came to fetch her, she had found Mary Catherine sitting on the playground, crying, while all the other first-grade girls skipped rope and chanted, "Mary Catherine Mac-in-tosh, Got no brains, oh my gosh!"

Mary Catherine never returned to school after that day. Now, more than 40 years later, she was still Miss Annie's little girl, and she was our favorite playmate.

The third resident of Miss Annie's household was Rachel. Her full name was Rattling Rachel, and she was a gray 1939 Chevrolet sedan with a sharply pointed nose and tiny round taillights shaped like gray torpedoes. Rachel lived in a wooden garage outside the kitchen door and separate from the rest of the house.

She was a wonderful car, with two gearshifts. In 1939 Rachel had been built by Chevrolet with a shift on the steering column and one of the first vacuum clutches ever used on one of her kind. Miss Annie said the clutch had burned up, though Joe-brother and I could find no evidence of a fire. Some forgotten dirt-road mechanic had pulled out not just the clutch but the entire transmission and replaced it with a second-hand transmission from a slightly older Chevy. The "new" transmission had a floor shift, which now came through a hole cut in the floorboard. A carpet scrap slipped down over the floor shift made a boot to cover the hole around the base and keep out the dirt and cold air.

The best part of the entire transmission transplant was that the old disconnected column shift was still there, right on the steering column. When we went to ride, I sat in Miss Annie's lap while she drove, and we each had a gearshift.

I would feel her left knee sink under my bottom as she pushed in the clutch. She would say, "Shift!" and I would throw the dead column shift into imaginary second gear while she slipped the floor shift up or down into the right place.

The five of us—Miss Annie, Mary Catherine, Rattling Rachel, Joe-brother, and I—spent afternoons and summer days in adventure around the big house. When things got dull, Miss Annie would say, "Let's shoot some Yankees!"

She'd go to the bottom drawer of her chest of drawers, take out the big Confederate battle flag, and thumbtack it to a broomstick. Mary Catherine always got to carry the flag. Miss Annie couldn't take a chance on one of us boys letting it drag on the ground.

We would run, led by Miss Annie and followed by Mary Catherine struggling with the flag, up and down hills, through the pastures, in and out of the woods, shooting at Yankees who surely had to be behind every bush and rock. Once we were fully exhausted, we would all drag back to the house, out of breath, to see how many times we had been "wounded."

Wounds were cockleburs, beggar-lice, and whatever other seeds and burs had clung to our clothes during the battle. A cocklebur counted as a cannonball fragment. Beggar-lice and smaller stickers were simple flesh wounds from some sniper's rifle. The winner of the battle was, of course, the one who had collected the greatest number of wounds and still lived.

When we went home each day, Mother would ask, "What did you boys do at Miss Annie's today?"

On this particular day we answered together, "We killed Yankees!"

"The country's safe for a while," Joe-brother added.

Mother looked at Daddy, pointed her finger at the side of her head, and as she rotated her finger in a gesture indicating a lack of all sense, said, "That woman . . . that woman is C-R-A-Z-Y!" She spelled out the last word slowly. But we always got to go back because Miss Annie was the only babysitter around.

One of the biggest reasons we liked to go to Miss Annie's on Saturdays and in the summertime was that, unlike on school days, we could arrive early enough to listen in as she read to Mary Catherine. We discovered the reading time one day when, on a trip to town, we stopped by the little public library and loaded Rachel's back seat with books. "What are all these books for?" Joe-brother asked Miss Annie.

"Oh, I like to read them to Mary Catherine," was the answer. We learned that each day, right after lunch, Miss Annie would read aloud to Mary Catherine for at least an hour, sometimes much longer. As often as possible Joe-brother and I began to join the party.

The first book I remember hearing her read was a small Dickens novel called *Dombey and Son*, a tragic story of failed possibilities. Miss Annie's favorites included Thomas Nelson Page's stories of the South. I especially remember *Two Little Confederates*.

My all-time favorite was a thick, square red book entitled *Beautiful Joe*. It was the sad story of a dog who had been abused by his cruel owner. But finally, even with his ears and tail cut off, poor Joe found a new home where he was deemed beautiful.

We loved reading time.

There was a small pond in Miss Annie's pasture that she called the cow pond. It was halfway between Rachel's garage and the Caldwells' barn, and though no fish lived there, it was a good place to throw rocks and sail boats.

After hearing Miss Annie read *The Adventures of Huckleberry Finn*, Joe-brother and I decided it would be a great thing to have a raft to float around on the cow pond. When we told Miss Annie about our idea, she said, "Go to it, boys. What do you need to build a raft?"

"Logs. Trees, I guess," I replied. Joe-brother agreed.

"How about those right there," she said, pointing to a stand of rough-barked black pines just below the garage. Miss Annie hunted around in the back of Rachel's garage until she came up with an old double-bitted ax, a hatchet, and a hand-saw. All three looked more like early-American antiques than usable tools.

So armed, Joe-brother and I set to work. In two days we managed to cut down a tall pine tree with a substantial, sappy trunk. After trimming off all the limbs, we sawed the trunk into two sections, each about 12 feet long. The plan had been—following Miss Annie's suggestions—to cut the trees and then assemble the raft in Rachel's garage, but now we discovered that we could not budge even half of the first log. Discouraged, we consulted Miss Annie.

"Rachel will do it," she replied. We watched as she tied one end of a long, thick rope to the pine log, ran the rope around a pole in the back of the garage, and then tied the other end to Rachel's bumper. After it was all hooked up, she drove Rachel down the driveway until we yelled, "Stop!" One more hook-up, and both pieces of the pine log were neatly in the garage.

Over the next two weeks Joe-brother and I managed to cut down enough black pines to end up with nine good-sized logs in Rachel's garage. We levered them into place side by side and then nailed a platform of boards across the top. The whole structure was completed with Coca-Cola crates for seats and a flagstaff on the front. The finished raft must have weighed close to a ton.

Joe-brother and I went to Miss Annie and asked for help. "The raft's all finished," we reported. "Now we need you and Rachel to help us get it down to the cow pond."

Miss Annie backed Rachel up to the garage and tied the raft to the back bumper. After considerable wheel-spinning on Rachel's part, the raft began to emerge from the garage and to travel in a cloud of dust toward the cow pond.

Miss Annie drove as close to the cow pond as she could. Still, we could not begin to budge the raft the last couple of feet to the water.

"Wait right here," she ordered. Again we watched as she drove Rachel to the other side of the cow pond, then pulled the long rope through the water as she walked back around to where we were. Once the rope was tied to the raft, she returned to the car.

"Stand back!" she ordered. The rope tightened, the wheels spun momentarily, and then the huge raft moved forward, launched on its maiden voyage in the cow pond. As soon as the sappy pine logs touched the water, the entire contraption sank straight to the bottom. All you could see was the tip of the flagstaff sticking up into the air. Rachel stopped abruptly, and Miss Annie, realizing what had happened, got out.

"Don't worry, boys," she shouted, as she untied the rope from Rachel's bumper. "It'll float to the top as soon as the logs dry out."

Joe-brother and I just looked at each other. We were both thinking the same thing. Was she really C-R-A-Z-Y the way Mother said? Or was this another mysterious case in which "People get what they deserve?" I guessed we weren't old enough to know.

Whenever Miss Annie was not babysitting us, her favorite pastime was growing flowers, summer and winter, indoors and out. During the warm months she dug and planted outside. There were jack-in-the-pulpits, trilliums, and ferns of various kinds at the edge of the yard and under the big hemlock trees. There were a rose garden and wide beds of annuals and perennials that served as a source of cut flowers throughout summer and into fall. My favorite section was a wide band of dahlias with blooms so big the plants had to be staked to hold them upright. Mother said that in spite of being C-R-A-Z-Y, Miss Annie surely did have a green thumb.

When the outdoor growing season was past, Miss Annie continued to grow flowers indoors with her needle and thread. Her finished products were beautiful pieces of crewel embroidery and cross-stitch samplers that looked like the fronts of candy boxes, with rows of ABC's running around the outside and flower arrangements in the center. Sometimes she created needlepoint pillow covers and chair cushions all covered with flowers.

197

Of all her needle-and-thread creations, the things Joe-brother and I loved most were what she called her "applied work" quilt tops. She would save scraps of every sort to get ready. Then she would lay out a huge solid-colored background, usually green, for the earth, with an occasional strip of blue for the sky. She cut the saved scraps into the shapes of animals and trees and houses and flowers. Miss Annie made calico cows and gingham mountains—whatever she thought of at the moment. The pieces were hemmed, placed, and sewed to the background, creating a beautiful, primitive scene of rural life, as she saw it. Joe-brother and I could watch her do "applied work" for hours.

Joe-brother and I never fought at Miss Annie's house but once. On that one occasion, we tried to have a little fight that we were both determined to finish as soon as it was started. Miss Annie, however, caught us before we had stopped.

"You want to fight?" she said.

"Oh, no," we answered in chorus. "We don't want to fight. We were just playing."

"No," she replied, "you were fighting. I saw you. If you want to fight, then we'll just find out about fighting. Hit him again, Joe."

She made us fight through most of the afternoon. Her instructions were, "Hit him again. No, hit him hard enough that I can see a red place where you hit him. Now you scratch him back, and I want to see the fingernail marks where you scratched. Now pull hair, and pull it *out* while you're at it. Now *bite*, and I'd better see tooth marks where you bite, or you'll just have to do it again . . ."

On and on we fought, wounded and exhausted, not allowed by Miss Annie to stop. While she gave the orders, she watched with tears running down her face, saying finally, "If old McKinley had only known . . . if old McKinley had only known what happens when you really fight, maybe things wouldn't have turned out the way they did."

After that, if we wanted to fight, we did it at home, where it was safe. Mother always stopped us. We wouldn't take a chance on another fight at Miss Annie's house.

One afternoon Miss Annie said, "Come on, boys, let's shoot down airplanes!" The Sulphur Springs Air Force was made up of two J-3 Piper Cubs and a yellow Stearman biplane that was flown in and out of Burgie Welch's hay field by a half-dozen local heroes who had learned to fly in the war. The hay field curved slightly, which made landings especially exciting, and the hangar was an old hay barn with an orange windsock on top.

Miss Annie took us to the top of a long hill, which overlooked the length of the hay field, and we got ready. We had come armed with an old .410 shotgun that Miss Annie always kept in the front closet, loaded with rat-shot. The loaded gun was kept, in her words, "to protect us from the roving element." She did occasionally fire it out the door when she'd heard strange noises in the night, and the noises usually stopped immediately.

It was years later that I realized we were at least a hundred yards from the landing strip and posed no real danger to the airplanes—or anything else there, for that matter. On top of the hill that day, though, we were deadly. We'd take turns loading the little single-shot gun with the rat-shot. Then when one of the airplanes (all painted the same color of yellow) came in for a landing, we would shoot—blam!—just as the wheels touched the ground. Of course, the airplane would stop after being shot, and Miss Annie would shout, "You got it!" We laid rows of sticks on the ground to keep score of how many we had each shot down.

We were doing so well that Joe-brother and I had both been declared "aces" when I said, "Miss Annie, I want to shoot one as it takes off."

"They're hard to hit when they take off," she said, "but you can try."

I reloaded the little shotgun and waited. Soon one of the yellow Piper Cubs taxied to the far end of the runway, turned around, and with a whooshing roar came down the field from right to left below us, tail off the ground and building speed fast. When the wheels were about 10 feet off the ground, I pulled the trigger. Blam! went the shotgun. At nearly the same time the Piper Cub's engine coughed, and the wooden propeller seemed to jump backwards and stop.

Silently the Piper Cub sank to the ground and bounced twice on its front wheels as the end of the hay field ran out. On the third bounce the landing gear caught the top of the hedgerow between the hay field and Daddy's garden, and as if in slow motion, the tail of the Cub came up and over, until the whole yellow airplane landed upside-down in the middle of Daddy's corn and bean patch.

I looked at Miss Annie. She was pale. The three of us started running down the hill toward the airplane. We stopped when we saw the doors pop open, as Willie Parker came out one side and Mr. Boyd came out the other. They began to walk around in the corn and examine the almost-undamaged airplane.

As soon as she realized that no one was hurt, Miss Annie looked at me and said, "You got it!" Then we headed back to her house—fast.

That afternoon Mary Catherine walked home with Joe-brother and me. Mother was standing in the door waiting for us when we got there. When we got close enough to hear, she said, "Do you know what happened? They were trying to take off in one of those crazy awful airplanes—you know they scare me to death—and the engine just cut off, and it ended up upside-down . . . "

She never got to finish her story because Joe-brother and I answered together, "We know."

"Miss Annie and I shot it down!" I said.

She turned quickly toward Daddy, finger pointed toward her head and already moving. "I told you," she said, "that woman is C-R-A-Z-Y!"

Mary Catherine was standing there watching the whole scene. Daddy hushed Mother quickly. "Don't say that in front of Mary Catherine, Mama."

"Oh, she doesn't know what that means. You know she can't read or write or anything." We thanked Mary Catherine for walking home with us, and she left, heading home more quickly than usual.

Whenever we stayed all day at Miss Annie's, she would put us down for an afternoon nap in an upstairs bedroom. There was a big high four-poster bed with a thick feather mattress on it. Miss Annie would put us on top of the bedspread and cover us with a quilt. One of us would always say, "Show us where the clock hands have to point before we can get up." She would go to the loudly ticking clock on the dresser and answer, "The short hand has to point to the four, and the long hand has to point to the 12."

Joe-brother and I would agree.

As soon as Miss Annie's footsteps had faded down the stairs, Joe-brother and I would jump up and turn the knobs on the back of the alarm clock until, indeed, the short hand was on the four and the long hand exactly on the 12. Then we would get up.

Miss Annie didn't care. All she needed was to be able to answer with an honest yes if Mother happened to ask her, "Did you put the boys down for a nap today?"

On one long summer afternoon Miss Annie put us down for a nap just as a thunderstorm came across Plott's Knob Mountain. Almost as soon as she left the room, Joe-brother and I jumped up and changed the clock.

Because the thunder and the rain made so much noise, we couldn't tell where in the big house Miss Annie might be. So we stayed in the bedroom and raised the shades to watch the storm.

When we looked out the window, we saw Miss Annie outside. She was walking around in the yard, in the rain, wearing only her normal cotton-print dress. She had no hat, no coat, not even an umbrella—but she seemed to enjoy the drenching the summer rain gave her as it poured down, punctuated by lightning and thunderclaps. She looked up and stretched her arms toward the falling rain.

I thought that the rain streaming down her face looked like rivers of tears. Then I realized that there might also be tears on her face, but in the rain no one would see them.

"Maybe she is C-R-A-Z-Y," Joe-brother whispered.

We decided not to tell our mother what we had seen. We might not get to come back anymore.

Later in the afternoon Miss Annie came to the bedroom, dry and in a fresh dress, to tell us it was time to get up.

The years rolled past, and gradually Joe-brother and I outgrew our need for a babysitter. Eventually our fascination with going to Miss Annie's house began to dull, and we seldom went there on our own anymore.

Miss Annie and Mary Catherine also got older, though Mary Catherine still seemed like a 7-year-old. More than once we overheard our parents talking about the two of them. "I wonder what poor Mary Catherine will do when Miss Annie's not there to take care of her anymore?"

Finally, Daddy would say, "You better check on them tomorrow, Mama."

Rattling Rachel was dead. Miss Annie had told us about her sudden death. "She was perfectly fine when we went to town on Tuesday, and then on Wednesday morning when I turned her on and pushed the starter button, she was dead. Oh, well, I guess she's run long enough—and I guess maybe I've driven long enough. Rachel deserves a rest."

With that, she swept out the inside of the car, washed and dried the outside, covered Rachel with clean sheets, and padlocked the garage door. We had never seen her do that before.

Then she took Rachel's keys, put them in an envelope with her oldest grandson's name on it, and placed them on the mantel in the living room. "He'll probably want to bring her back to life someday."

Mother now became Miss Annie and Mary Catherine's chauffeur. The call would come in midmorning: "Could you take me to see Dr. York?" Joe-brother and I would ride along, as did Mary Catherine, while we went to town and waited for Miss Annie to be finished at Dr. York's office.

It was never straight home, though, as Miss Annie would ask—one stop at a time—to go to the church, the library, the circle president's house, the home of the secretary of the D.A.R., the drug store, and finally the grocery store.

It would be well after dark before we returned home, and Mother would be furious. Our supper was still to be fixed before we could even begin to go to bed.

Daddy would try to calm her down. "You have to take her places, Mama. After all, she helped us raise the boys."

Miss Annie didn't die all at once. She simply faded from action one part at a time. First her legs failed, and she could no longer work in the yard or maintain the flower beds. The wildflowers didn't care: they just got wilder and wilder, and gradually there was less and less lawn to mow, as they took over the yard.

Still, she grew her needlework flowers and assembled her applied-work worlds until her eyes failed. Even then she tried to do it by touch, but the stems would come out in one place and the blooms in another, and Miss Annie eventually gave it up.

She spent most of her days in bed, and occasionally Joe-brother and I would go to her house. Now we'd read to her. Again and again she'd ask to hear *Two Little Confederates* and *Beautiful Joe*. Tears ran down all our faces, Mary Catherine's too, as we read about the poor earless dog until the book fell apart.

People who had worried for years about Mary Catherine gradually began to realize that she had become the mother, as Miss Annie had become the child, and that she could, in fact, take care of herself very well.

Finally, when she was 97 years old, Miss Annie's heart stopped, and as suddenly as Rachel had died, she was gone. The day after Miss Annie was buried in Cedar Hill Cemetery, Mary Catherine called our mother, and said, "All of you come up here." It was an order not to be ignored. "Mother left something she said I was supposed to give you when she died."

We got in the blue Dodge and drove up to the old, now failing house. Rachel's road was badly washed out, the yard had long gone unmowed, the porch was rotten in spots, and the paint was badly peeled. "I didn't realize what kind of shape this place was in," Daddy said as we knocked on the door.

Mary Catherine let us in and led us to the dining room. Above the dining-room table was a chandelier that had seven light bulbs. Miss Annie had always kept all but one unscrewed. When Mary Catherine reached up and screwed in the other six, the room blazed with light, and we knew we had come for something important.

"Stay here," she ordered as she retreated into Miss Annie's bedroom. Joe-brother and I saw her fumbling in the bottom drawer of the dresser. We knew the Confederate flag stayed there—maybe that was going to be for us. We had always wanted it.

Mary Catherine ignored the flag and removed a huge package wrapped in brown paper. She carried it to the dining-room table and began to unwrap the parcel with great and deliberate care. There on the table in front of us began to unfold the biggest applied-work quilt we had ever seen.

The background was earth and sky and mountains. There was a big ridiculous-looking white Victorian house in the center, with a pointed roof and a lightning rod (blue glass ball and all) on the peak.

On the porch was the figure of a girl holding a Confederate flag on what looked for all the world like a broomstick. There were a gray car at the side, a yellow airplane overhead, and flowers everywhere.

Through the yard in front of the house raced two little boys. Between them was an old lady, gray-haired, with her hands stretched out and her fingers just touching the tops of their heads. At the bottom of it all, in big block letters, we read the words MY BOYS.

Mother began to cry. "Why did she do it?" she said. "*How* did she do it . . . with those old fingers? Why, she has grandchildren of her own. Why did she do this for us?"

Daddy tried to save the day. "Oh, Mama, you know why she did it. She said it herself. 'People get what they deserve.' Isn't that right, Mary Catherine?"

Mary Catherine didn't hesitate for a moment but very quickly and firmly said, "No. That isn't why she did it at all. She did it because she was C-R-A-Z-Y!"

Donald Davis grew up in a family of storytellers who have lived on the same Western North Carolina land since 1781. A former Methodist minister, now a performer and teacher, Davis has told his original stories to audiences since 1980. He lives in Ocracoke, North Carolina.

THE SWORD OF WOOD

Doug Lipman

Jewish variants of this worldwide folk tale emphasize creativity and faith—qualities that male heroes often subordinate to strength and skill. Now, as the survival of human life seems to depend on our finding ways to circumvent violent conflict, this old story seems more timely than ever. My version is recorded on Milk From the Bull's Horn: Tales of Nurturing Men *(Yellow Moon Press).*

There was once a king who loved nothing better than to go out alone at night in the clothes of a commoner. He wanted to meet the ordinary people of his kingdom—to learn their way of life and especially their way of thinking about the world.

One night this king found himself walking in the poorest, narrowest street of the city. This was the street of the Jews. He heard a song in the distance. The king thought, *A song sung in this place of poverty must be a lament.* But as he got closer, he could hear the true character of the song: it was a song of pride! "Bai-yum-dum, bai-yum-bai, yum-bai, bai . . . "

The king was drawn to the source of the song: the smallest, humblest shack on the street. He knocked on the door. "Is a stranger welcome here?"

The voice from within said, "A stranger is God's gift. Come in."

In the dim light inside, the king saw a man sitting on his only piece of furniture, a wooden box. When the king came in, the man stood up and sat on the floor, offering the king the crate for a seat.

"Well, my friend," the king asked, "what do you do to earn a living?"

"Oh, I am a cobbler."

"You have a shop where you make shoes?"

"Oh, no, I could not afford a shop. I take my box of tools—you are sitting on it—to the side of the road. There I repair shoes for people as they need them."

"You cobble shoes by the side of the road? Can you make enough money that way?"

The cobbler spoke with both humility and pride. "Every day I make just enough money to buy food for that day."

"Just enough for one day? Aren't you afraid that one day you won't make enough, and then you'll go hungry?"

"Blessed be the One who carries us day by day."

The next day the king determined to put this man's philosophy to the

206

test. He issued a proclamation that anyone wishing to cobble shoes by the side of the road must purchase a license for 50 pieces of gold.

That night the king returned to the street of the Jews. Again he heard a song in the distance, and thought, *This time, the cobbler will be singing a different tune.* But when the king neared the house, he heard the cobbler sing the same song. In fact, it was even longer, with a new phrase that soared joyfully: "Ah, ha-ah-ah, ah-ha, ah-ha, ah-yai."

The king knocked on the door. "Oh, my friend, I heard about that wicked king and his proclamation. I was so worried about you. Were you able to eat today?"

"Oh, I was angry when I heard I could not make my living in the way I always have. But I knew: I am entitled to make a living, and I will find a way. As I stood there, saying those very words to myself, a group of people passed me by. When I asked them where they were going, they told me: into the forest to gather firewood. Every day they bring back wood to sell as kindling. When I asked if I could join them, they said, 'There is a whole forest out there. Come along!'

"So I gathered firewood. At the end of the day I was able to sell it for just enough money to buy food for today."

The king sputtered, "Just enough for one day? What about tomorrow? What about next week?"

"Blessed be the One who carries us day by day."

The next day the king again returned to his throne and issued a new proclamation: That anyone caught gathering firewood in the royal forest would be inducted into the royal guard. For good measure he issued another: No new members of the royal guard would be paid for 40 days.

That night the king returned to the street of the Jews. Amazed, he heard the same song! But now it had a third part that was militant and determined: "Dee, dee, dee, dee-dee, dee-dee, da . . . "

The king knocked on the door. "Cobbler, what happened to you today?"

"They made me stand at attention all day in the royal guard. They issued me a sword and a scabbard. But then they told me I wouldn't be paid for 40 days!"

"Oh, my friend, I bet you wish now that you had saved some money."

"Well, let me tell you what I did. At the end of the day I looked at that metal sword blade. I thought to myself, *That must be valuable*. So I removed the blade from the handle and fashioned another blade of wood. When the sword is in the scabbard, no one can tell the difference. I took the metal blade to a pawnbroker, and I pawned it for just enough money to buy food for one day."

The king was stunned. "But what if there's a sword inspection tomorrow?"

"Blessed be the One who carries us day by day."

The next day the cobbler was pulled out of line in the king's guard and was presented with a prisoner in chains.

"Cobbler, this man has committed a horrible crime. You are to take him to the square. Using your sword, you are to behead him."

"Behead him? I'm an observant Jew. I couldn't take another human life."

"If you do not, we'll kill both of you."

The cobbler led the trembling man into the square, where a crowd had gathered to watch the execution, and put the prisoner's head on the chopping block. He stood tall, his hand on the handle of his sword. Facing the crowd, he spoke.

"Let God be my witness: I am no murderer! If this man is guilty as charged, let my sword be as always. But if he is innocent, let my sword turn to wood!"

He pulled his sword. The people gasped when they saw the wooden blade, and they bowed down at the great miracle that had taken place there.

The king, who had been watching all of this, came over to the cobbler. He took him by the hand and looked him deep in the eyes. "I am the king. And I am also your friend who has visited you these last several nights. I want you to come live with me in the palace and be my advisor. Please teach me how to live as you do—one day at a time."

Then, in front of everyone, the two of them danced and sang: "Bai-yum-dum, bai-yum-bai, yum-bai, bai . . . "

Doug Lipman, a former nursery school and music teacher, has been a professional storyteller since 1975. Noted for his telling of Jewish and participatory folk tales, Lipman is considered one of the foremost storytelling coaches in the country. He lives in West Somerville, Massachusetts.

THE GIRL AND THE GHOST

Laura Simms

For the past 10 years I have told this Nisqualli tale to adults and older children with the same effect—total immersion and silence. "Is it true?" I'm often asked. "Yes," I answer. "Didn't you see it?"

On an island in the Northwest there lived a chief who had three beautiful daughters. "This is my true wealth," he boasted. He became very rich from the marriages of his two elder girls and said to his wife, "Our youngest daughter is more lovely than the older ones. She could fetch an even greater bride price." Young men traveled from far and wide to seek her hand, but the chief turned them away, saying, "Their offerings are too small."

The village was remote and had enjoyed years of peace and prosperity. No one lacked fish or seal, and the people were protected by ancient myth and custom. Their homes sat safely between earth and sky and sea. They had had no complaint with the chief, but now the old people warned him, "Your desire is unnatural. It will bring only disaster and unhappiness." He mocked them for their belief in old tales, saying, "You spend too much time listening to ghost stories and gossip. Times have changed."

One night the chief and his wife were awakened by the sound of singing. The most enchanting voices filled the night air. By the time they were dressed and standing outside, finely carved canoes had pulled to their shore.

A noble young man stood before all the other strangers. He wore a blanket adorned with turquoise, feathers, and beads. His black hair shone like silk. Behind him were painted boxes, piles of blankets, copper trinkets, feathered capes, baskets, silver, bowls, and skins.

The stranger approached, offering an elegant greeting to the chief, his wife, and the daughter. Then he asked for the young woman's hand in marriage. She watched, impressed by his dignity and language. The chief, seeing the abundance of gifts, agreed to the wedding.

"I am honored," said the stranger. "And I ask that the wedding be held tonight since I must return to my own people before dawn."

The chief had the people awakened, although it was the middle of the night, and the bonfires were lit. Food was cooked. Dances and songs were performed, and gifts were exchanged. And before sunrise the handsome bridegroom sat with his new bride by his side in the largest canoe and rowed away from the island.

Everyone in the village was entranced by the beautiful singing and stood on the shore until the wedding party had vanished in the distance. Only then did the chief's wife say, as if arising from a dream, "We never asked the name of the land where our daughter is going."

"Do not worry," the chief assured her. "They will return when their first child is born, as is the custom." The chief was satisfied with his new-found wealth and slept deeply.

Meanwhile the young bride sat beside her new husband. She was filled with joy, imagining the life they would lead together. Her husband and his people were friendly, and their songs were more wonderful than any she had heard in her village.

Then in the shadowy mist of the first light of dawn, she saw an island appear, like the back of a seal rising out of the water. The voices that greeted them were joyful. Young women her own age helped her onto the land and led her to her house. A hundred people made a path for them to walk through. She saw children in circles playing games and old people laughing and gossiping in the distance.

When she yawned, her husband took her hand and whispered, "We can sleep all day, and in the evening I will tell you all you need to know about this land."

The house she entered was new. She smelled sweet cedar and noticed beautiful baskets and shiny pots. The blanket on their bed was red and yellow and blue. The two lay down to rest beneath it, and no sooner did she put her head on his shoulder than she drifted into sleep. He caressed her hair and said, "It has been a long journey."

She wasn't accustomed to sleeping during the day, and when the sun was bright, she opened her eyes. It was unearthly quiet. Startled, she sat up. Light streamed though broken walls. The pots were tarnished, and a musty smell filled the air. The baskets she had admired had unraveled, and the blanket was faded. Only then did she realize that the body lying next to her was icy cold. Turning, she stared into the empty sockets of a skull.

She tried to scream, but no sound issued forth. As she moved away from the skull, it fell to the side with a click. Frantic, she threw open the door to seek help.

She saw only white sand and yellowing bones. Skeletons everywhere. No flesh, no faces—only bones. She stepped over the dead carefully and raced to the shore. Leaping over the corpses lying there, she took hold of a canoe and shoved it into the water. But it moved through her fingers like a feather, dissolving like moth-eaten cloth.

"There must be a living person on this land somewhere," she assured herself. "Surely there must be someone in this place." Scanning the shore, she saw nothing. Then in the distance she made out a house with smoke rising.

She stepped cautiously among the skeletons and walked toward the house. Yet the further she walked, the more distant it seemed. At first she was careful of the bones, but when fear gripped her again, she grew careless, stepping on the bodies, kicking the bones to the left and the right. The cracking bones pierced the silence like the cry of a gull.

By late afternoon she stood before a house. Its small door opened, but no one greeted her. Slowly she went in. In the dim light she saw an ancient woman as small as a child, sitting in the middle of the room, weaving blankets with her own hair. Her eyes were large, and her face was lined with wrinkles.

The girl sobbed, but the woman said, "My name is Screech Owl Woman. I will not harm you. You must be the one our chief married in the night."

"I want to go home," the girl stuttered.

"Why are you awake in the daylight?" asked the Old One, putting down her weaving.

"Please," the girl begged, "Let me go home."

Screech Owl woman motioned her closer. "They should have told you where you are. This is the land of the dead, and your husband is the chief of ghosts."

The young woman closed her eyes and moaned, "I am not dead."

"You can't go home now," the old woman said softly. "When you learn about the land of the dead, you will not be unhappy. Sit beside me, and I will tell you all you need to know about the laws of this land. Here things are reversed from the ways of the world of the living. But this land is not evil. The ghosts are charming, and your husband is the most kind of all."

The girl sat down, and Screech Owl Woman described the land of the dead and the rules that bound the ghosts to that world. Slowly the young woman from the land of the living grew less afraid.

As time passed, it began to grow dark. She heard voices, beautiful voices singing, and she knew that the ghosts were taking back their skins. At first the voices sounded friendly. But as they grew louder, a chill ran up her spine. "They are coming for me," she gasped.

The footsteps of the ghosts racing on the sand pounded like a hundred drums. They were calling for Screech Owl Woman to give them the girl.

"She has killed many ghosts!" shouted one.

"Many have lost their arms or their legs," complained another.

A third wailed, "Her husband's head has been twisted to one side."

The Old One went to the door. The girl begged her not to give her back to them. But she blinked and nodded for the girl to follow.

At the sight of Screech Owl Woman, the ghosts grew still. "It is your fault," she reprimanded the ghosts, as if they were her children. "You should have told her where she was. Have no anger. I have instructed her, and now she can return peacefully to her husband.

"I am always here," Screech Owl Woman said to the girl. Reluctantly, the wife of the chief returned with the ghosts.

The house was as it had been the night before. Everything was new. Her husband lay beneath the many-colored blanket and wore a bandage around his neck. He smiled, and she placed her cool hand on his forehead to comfort him. Gladly, then, she sat beside him.

It wasn't long before she grew accustomed to sleeping during the day and being awake at night. She learned to live among the ghosts and grew to love her husband.

Everything was fine until she gave birth to a baby. The ghosts didn't like her son. "He is neither child nor ghost," they complained. At last the chief of the ghosts decided to take her back to her homeland.

One night he laid his son on a wooden board and covered him with 12 cloths. "Take the boy to the land of your parents," he said sadly. "He will live the life of a human child, and in time he will know death, but I will not know him again. You must promise that no one will look upon his face for 12 days and 12 nights. Then he will be a child. If he is seen, I will return for you, and he will be a ghost forever."

The princess embraced her husband and promised to follow his instructions. Then she took the strange bundle in her arms, and that night they paddled back to this world.

In the land of the living the moon was full. The chief and his wife awoke again to the sound of singing and remarked, "They have returned." The chief's wife could not hide her joy and said, "She holds a baby."

But upon the couple's arrival the girl stepped solemnly out of the canoe, and the husband turned and left without saying a word.

"Mother, Father," the girl said slowly, "you married me to the chief of the ghosts, and I have lived in the land of the dead."

That night she explained why they could not see their grandchild for 12 days and 12 nights. They stayed awake until dawn, and she described the world of the ghosts and how they lived during the night.

She was glad to be home, and the days passed quickly. Once again she became accustomed to sleeping in the nighttime and being awake during the day. She rarely went outside. Mainly she sat with the baby on her knees and rocked him, singing songs from both worlds.

But as the days passed, she grew lonely for company. Finally, on the morning of the 12th day, she asked her mother to watch the child while she visited with a friend. "In a few hours we can see his face. Then my son will be like other children," she said, and she departed cheerfully.

The grandmother took the baby on her knees as her daughter had done day after day and rocked him back and forth, singing songs that had been sung to her as a child and songs she had sung to her daughters.

Then she said to herself, "How strange this is. No one has ever seen the face of a ghost, and I am holding a ghost from the land of the dead. What a pity that we will never know how they look." The baby cooed and giggled, and the grandmother held him closer. "In just a few hours he will be like every other child." Then she said, "What harm would it be if I just looked quickly? Then we would know how they appear. No one need fear. I will barely look at his face."

As quiet as a cloud, she shut the door and took off the first cloth. The baby moved. "Hush, little prince," she whispered, and she took off the second cloth. She removed the third and fourth. The baby grew still. She lifted the fifth and the sixth. "You are quiet, my little one," she hummed. She removed the seventh and eighth and ninth cloths. The bundle grew lighter. Then she took off the 10th, and a chill breeze swept under the door into the room. With hands trembling, she took off the 11th cloth. "One more, my little man," she said, and she slowly grasped the edge of the cloth and removed it from his face.

Screaming, she dropped the bundle to the floor. A tiny skeleton shattered, bits of it flying in every direction, and worms and maggots crawled between the bones.

At that very instant the girl fell ill. She left the house of her friend and ran to her mother's lodge. She opened the door, then fell to the floor and began to gather up the bones of her baby. Weeping, she placed them on the board in the shape of the boy and gently touched each one. Then she covered him again with the cloths. "Mother, why did you look?" she said, with pity but no anger, and taking the baby, she left the house.

As the sun went down, she heard her husband singing. Her father and mother stood by their house in silence, side by side, and watched as she returned to the land of the dead.

That night her son became a ghost, and she, in time, became a ghost as well. She returned to the land of the living only one more time, but she never touched the earth.

When the boy was 3 years old, on the night of a full moon, she rowed out to sea, singing. She held the child up in the moonlight for the chief and his wife to see.

Since that time no one has traveled from the land of the dead to the land of the living. And no one has gone from this world to that. No one, that is, except old Screech Owl Woman, who still travels back and forth but is never seen in her human form. You can still hear her eerie song at night, and sometimes you can see her shadow in the moonlight.

Laura Simms, a professional storyteller since 1968, has achieved interna-tional recognition as a performer and a spokeswoman for the oral tradition. A New York City–based author and recording artist, Simms is currently performing the one-woman show "Long Journey Home" and writing a novel based on her childhood in Brooklyn.

No News

The Folktellers
Connie Regan-Blake and Barbara Freeman

A certain Southern lady was returning home after recuperating in the mountains for three months. Her friend Georgeanne met her at the railway-station platform.

"Georgeanne, has there been any news while I've been away?"

"Oh, no, there hasn't been any news."

"Surely something must have occurred in my absence. Why, I've been gone for three months, and I'm anxious for any little bit of news you may have."

"Well, now that you mention it—of course, it don't amount to much. Since you've been away, your dog died."

"My dog died? How did my dog die?"

"He ate some of the burnt horseflesh."

"Burnt horseflesh?"

"After the fire cooled off, he went over and ate some of the burnt horseflesh, and that's what killed the dog."

"After the fire cooled off?"

"See, the barn burned down."

"My barn burned down? How did my barn burn down?"

"It was a spark from the house."

"A spark from the house?"

"Oh, yes, now, that's completely burned down."

"How did my house burn down?"

"See, it was the candles. They kind of lit up the curtains . . . "

"Candles? I don't even allow candles in the house. How did candles get in the house?"

"They was around the coffin."

"The coffin? Who died?"

"Now, you needn't worry about that. Since you've been away, your mother-in-law died."

"My mother-in-law. Oh, what a pity. Now how did she die?"

Early in our career we often performed with Marshall Dodge, a brilliant storyteller from Maine. He was telling "No News"—a story made popular by Nat M. Wills at the turn of the century. Marshall thought our tandem style was perfect for the story and encouraged us to add it to our repertoire. We have since shared it with untold numbers of listeners.

"Well, some folks say it was from the shock of hearing that your husband had run away with the choir leader. But other than that, there ain't been no news."

The Folktellers—Barbara Freeman and Connie Regan-Blake—directed storytelling programs at a public library before becoming full-time traveling storytellers in 1975. Pioneers of the art of telling in tandem, the two created and continue to perform Mountain Sweet Talk, *a two-act play about the importance of stories in our lives. They live in Asheville, North Carolina.*

THE WISE SHOEMAKER OF STUDENA

Syd Lieberman

Yossi was a shoemaker in the little village of Studena in Hungary. He was good at mending shoes, but he was even better at giving advice. Every day the villagers would crowd into his shop, asking for Yossi's opinion about one problem or another. Some days he talked more than he worked.

Word of the wise shoemaker of Studena spread throughout the land, and soon rich men and even noblemen from all over Hungary began to visit Yossi. They would squeeze into his little shop in Studena and fight over the privilege of just a moment of his time.

This is why Samuel, one of the richest merchants in Budapest, decided that he must get Yossi to attend his daughter's wedding. Samuel was a man who liked to show off. He had the finest house, the best clothes, and the largest belly of any merchant in town. *All my friends will envy me*, he thought. *I'll be the first man in Budapest to host the wise shoemaker of Studena.*

Samuel had never met Yossi, but he sent the shoemaker a long letter that praised his wisdom and begged him to come to the wedding. The wise shoemaker was delighted. He had always dreamed of going to the big city. Yossi closed the shop immediately and ran home to tell his wife the good news. "But what will you wear to such a wedding?" asked his wife. "Even your best clothes aren't good enough."

Yossi just smiled. "Why should I worry about what I wear? A goat has a beard, but that doesn't make him a rabbi."

It was a long trip to Budapest, but Yossi was so excited he hardly noticed. The city turned out to be even more grand than he had imagined—with so many people and such big buildings. Yossi craned his neck in all directions as he walked. Suddenly, he tripped on the cobblestone street and fell into a mud puddle. "What would my wife say now?" he said to himself when he found that he was covered with mud and one of his sleeves was ripped. "I will have to apologize to my host."

I wrote this story after reading Italian, Syrian, and Jewish versions of the tale, and I set it in my 82-year-old great-aunt's native village. She was present the first time I told the story and was very excited to hear the name of her hometown. After the program she came up to me to tell me how much she liked the story. "But," she added, "I don't think I knew that shoemaker."

219

Now, Samuel was greeting guests, and as he looked down the street, he saw a man coming toward him in clothes that were ripped and covered with mud. The wealthy merchant thought, *That man's a beggar. I don't want any beggars here*. So before Yossi could get a word out, Samuel shouted, "Away with you! My daughter is getting married today, and I'm expecting a very important man soon—the wisest man in all the land. I don't want him to see any beggars here." With that, Samuel took Yossi by the shoulders, spun him around, and pushed him out into the street.

"Hmm," Yossi said to himself, "Is this the man who says he loves wisdom? He's not very smart; I will have to teach him a lesson." And he strode off to find the home of a rich merchant who had visited him in Studena the week before.

When the rich man heard Yossi's story, he agreed to help teach Samuel a lesson. The merchant opened the door to his large wardrobe and invited Yossi to take his finest clothes. Yossi changed into purple velvet pants and a white Italian silk shirt with ruffles in the front. He pulled brown leather boots up to his knees and donned a gold and silver brocade coat. Then the merchant placed a large black fur hat on Yossi's head.

This time when Samuel saw Yossi coming, he thought, *That must be the shoemaker. Look how wonderfully he's dressed. I knew he was a great man*. Samuel greeted Yossi with respect, took him by the hand, and introduced him to all the guests. After the wedding ceremony Samuel seated Yossi in a place of honor, right next to the bride and groom.

Then wine was served, and Samuel rose and toasted the new couple. "To your health and happiness." Everyone stood and drank the wine. That is, everyone but Yossi. He stood, pulled his trousers away from his body, and poured the wine down his pants.

Everyone was amazed, and some laughed. But this was the wise shoemaker of Studena, so no one said a word.

The whole meal was like that. Yossi poured the chicken soup into his boot and swished it around. He smeared carrots up and down his arms, pushed potatoes into his shirt, and carefully spooned peas into his hat. Finally, Yossi placed cabbage balls in the pockets of his coat and squashed them. No one knew what to say or do. Of course, some of the children tried to imitate him, but they didn't get very far.

Samuel finally had had enough when Yossi held up a piece of apple strudel, smiled, and mashed it against his chest. "What are you doing?" Samuel shouted. "I invited you here to honor my daughter. You are known for your wisdom. But instead of speaking wisely or teaching us anything, you are acting like a madman."

"Oh," said Yossi, looking startled, "but I have been teaching you ever since we started eating. You see, I was that man you threw out earlier. You thought I was a beggar because of the way I was dressed. When I returned, dressed in the clothes of a rich man, you treated me with honor and respect. It seems you didn't really want me here at all. You just wanted my clothes. So I am feeding them." And with that, he poured a cup of tea into his pocket. "Drink well, my coat," he said. And then he left.

The next day Yossi sat in his home, eating breakfast and thinking about the wedding. "So," said his wife as she entered, sweeping the floor, "was I right about your clothes?"

Yossi laughed and took the broom out of her hand. He examined it at arm's length and then danced with it a step or two. "You know, even this broom would look good," he said with a wink, "if you dressed it up. Fools see men's clothes; wise men see their souls."

Syd Lieberman, a storyteller and teacher, collects, preserves, and tells the stories of his Jewish tradition—including family tales of growing up in Chicago. His story recordings have won many awards. Lieberman lives in Evanston, Illinois.

Index of Stories

Index of Tellers